BUILDING BRIDGES
NOT WALLS

s is an international Christian organization. Our mission is to reach, disciple, and equip w Christ and to make Him known through successive generations. We envision multitudes ple in the United States and every other nation who have a passionate love for Christ, live naring Christ's love, and multiply spiritual laborers among those without Christ.

e publishing ministry of The Navigators. NavPress publications help believers learn biblical ly what they learn to their lives and ministries. Our mission is to stimulate spiritual forma- ur readers.

ffery L. Rosenau

BRINGING TRUTH TO LIFE, and the NAVPRESS logo are registered trademarks of sence of ® in connection with marks of NavPress or other parties does not indicate an gistration of those marks.

3-394-1

by Dan Jamison
m: Paul Santhouse, Eric Stanford, Darla Hightower, Pat Miller

anecdotal illustrations in this book are true to life and are included with the permission of nvolved. All other illustrations are composites of real situations, and any resemblance to or dead is coincidental.

quotations in this publication are taken from the HOLY BIBLE: NEW INTERNATIONAL (NIV®). Copyright © 1973, 1978, 1984 by International Bible Society. Used by permission n Publishing House. All rights reserved.

he United States of America

7 8 9 10 / 07 06 05 04 03

FOR A FREE CATALOG OF
NAVPRESS BOOKS & BIBLE STUDIES,
CALL 1-800-366-7788 (USA)
OR 1-416-499-4615 (CANADA)

BUILDING [
NOT W[

LEARNING TO DIALOGUE IN T[

J E F F   R O S [

The Navigator[
people to kno[
of diverse peo[
a lifestyle of s[

NavPress is th[
truth and app[
tion among o[

© 2003 by Je[
All rights res[
sion from Na[
www.navpres[

NAVPRESS,[
NavPress. Ab[
absence of re[

ISBN 1-576[

Cover desig[
Creative Tea[

Some of the[
the persons[
people livin[

All Scriptur[
VERSION©[
of Zonderv[

Printed in t[

1 2 3 4 5 6[

NAVPRES[

Bringing Truth to Lif[
P.O. Box 35001, Colorado Springs, [

CONTENTS

ACKNOWLEDGMENTS

Thanks go to Cyndi Philkill for clearly seeing the vision God has given for this project. I greatly appreciate the countless hours you have devoted, Cyndi. Your love for the Lord and your skills in training and writing supplied what had been missing to make this an effective teaching tool. Thank you for sharing your talents.

Thanks also go to my friend Don Reeverts. Don, you have been a great encouragement along the way. Thank you for "speaking the truth in love" to me. It was a significant turning point in the development of *Building Bridges*.

Thank you to those who have prayed with me over the years: Art and Audrey, Jim and Kaye, Mary, Don, Pastor Chuck, Wayne, Edith and De Wayne, Aunt Ernestine, Jan, Lisa, Pastor Clyde, Jean, Gary, Dave, Chick, Pastor Doug, Pastor Ken, and Pastor Willie. You have helped me learn the power of prayer.

And special thanks to Bob, Dave, Steve, and Rusty of The Navigators.

Finally, I thank my two sons, Rob and Travis. Next to Jesus, you two guys are my best friends. You have watched me fail and learn, fail and learn for many years. You have seen me speak the truth and forget to love, and you have seen me attempt to love and then forget the truth. You have grown with me as we've learned together our desperate need to fall in love with Jesus Christ and abide in Him. Rob and Travis, thank you for your patience, for your understanding, and for the godly counsel you have given me over the years. I have great respect and much love for you and am forever grateful that God has blessed me with such sons.

INTRODUCTION

I know all about building walls. At one time wall building came naturally to me. In fact, I had erected a number of walls, isolating myself from people I disagreed with, before I even realized there was a problem with what I was doing. I had to go back to engineering school, so to speak, to learn how to build bridges that would enable authentic, helpful communication to travel back and forth between me and others.

Can you relate to this?

Perhaps you are having a disagreement with your spouse or some other family member or friend, and when you try to talk it out, the situation only seems to get worse. Perhaps you have taken up the noble challenge of trying to correct injustice or oppose immorality in society, but you find yourself alienating, rather than influencing, those who hold views different from your own. Perhaps in your church or workplace you rub shoulders with one who is very different from you in terms of ethnic background, political affiliation, or religious belief, and your relationship with that person has over time declined to the level of a cold hostility. These are only a few of the many possible scenarios in which people may fail to communicate productively.

We all find ourselves in a potentially antagonistic relationship from time to time. What do we do about it? I can attest from personal experience that it *is* possible to learn how to communicate constructively. It is possible to move from talking *at* or *about* another to talking *with* another. Allow me to tell you the story of how this wall builder learned to put his tools to a different use.

HOW I LEARNED TO BUILD BRIDGES

It was 1993, in the thick of the "culture wars," and I was eager to be a cultural warrior. I had been listening as political figures, celebrities, and media spokespersons set a tone for morality and truth in American society that offended the biblical values I held dear. I occupied no political office, no position of great influence. I was simply a father and the leader of a fledgling ministry. But I sensed that something was very wrong in the land I loved, and I felt a desire deep within me to do something to counteract the disturbing trends I was seeing. So I prayed, asking God to show me just one issue where I could get involved and have a positive influence.

God answered that prayer: sex education. This was a critical matter and one that I had a personal connection with, as my own two sons were taking a sex-ed class in high school. When I examined the material in their textbook, I saw that it came across as being unopposed to promiscuity and indifferent to the option of sexual abstinence before marriage. This concerned me. My own boys were sufficiently grounded in biblical principles to recognize falsehood, I believed, but what about the countless other students sitting in sex-ed classrooms across the country? I had my issue!

I began, I think, responsibly. For several weeks, I researched national guidelines on sex education. Furthermore, I spent close to a year evaluating hundreds of pages of textbooks used at the elementary, middle, and high school levels across the land and especially in my own state of Colorado. At the end, I was convinced that students were being taught philosophies of sexuality that were unhealthy and that ran counter to God's plan for sexuality. I was prepared to fight.

I began by meeting one-to-one with people who helped make decisions regarding what would be taught about sexuality in public-school health classes. I spoke with teachers and the principal at my sons' high school. Then I expanded my activities by speaking with health coordinators, members of the Colorado State Board of Education, and Colorado legislators. Most of these people, I found, would listen politely in one-to-one sessions, and a few even agreed to do what they could to make changes in Colorado's sex education.

So far, so good. The problem came when I started making my views known in public forums.

I began to attend parent gatherings, where I would stand up and "preach" about the evils of the current sex-education guidelines. I would also help other parents be prepared to discuss the issue with others. In all of this, I was critical and judgmental, not only of the national guidelines and state curricula, but also of the motives of the leaders within the sponsoring organizations. My words were heated, personal, and unkind. Now, I ask you: do you think I was building walls or bridges at this time? Walls—twenty feet high!

Fortunately, at that time I had a wise friend and mentor, Don Reeverts, who was (and still is) president of the Denver Leadership Foundation. I would meet with Don occasionally and keep him informed about my fight to change sex education. Don was supportive of my goal, but as time went on, his reaction to me changed. One day, as I was spewing my contempt of the system I was opposing, Don surprised me by focusing not on what I was doing but on how I was doing it. He commented, "All you want to do is fight."

It was a simple enough statement, and it was offered in a humble manner. But as I left my friend's office that day, I asked myself, *Is it true? Is fighting all I want to do?* I answered myself, too. *Yes, I want to fight! What's wrong with that? Truth is worth fighting for.* I pictured myself as one of the Old Testament warrior heroes, a Gideon or a Joshua, fighting for God's side. Nevertheless, God used my friend's simple words to show me that something inside me was not right.

Instead of the Old Testament warriors, another biblical figure—the greatest of them all—came to my mind: Jesus. How did my motives and actions appear when ranged alongside His? I opened my New Testament. There I was reminded that Jesus was "gentle and humble in heart" and would "not quarrel or cry out" (Matthew 11:29; 12:19). Moreover, Jesus Himself said, "My kingdom is not of this world. If it were, my servants would fight" (John 18:36). The apostle Paul instructed, "The Lord's servant must not quarrel; instead, he must be kind to everyone" and advised Christians to "[speak] the truth in love" (2 Timothy 2:24; Ephesians 4:15). All this brought me to humble myself.

The irony is that I had asked God to show me something that was a problem in society, and all the while, *I* was the problem. Here I was, a forgiven child of God being angry and critical of people who were no worse than I was, apart from the unmerited grace I had received. I viewed my adversaries as being deceived by the Adversary of us all and in need of Jesus Christ, but I had no compassion for them in my heart.

Since the start of my sex-ed battle, I had been looking at those on the other side as people who were beyond the reach of my love. But the truth was, no matter how wrong they were, they were not beyond the reach of God's love. I remembered Norma McCorvey, the "Roe" in "Roe v. Wade," whom God had wooed and won. God loved my opponents just as much as He loved Norma—or me, for that matter.

With these realizations, my mind-set changed completely. I began to see people through the eyes of Jesus. I started to care about people who had been deceived and led astray. I felt compassion for the people God loved and wanted to set free with the truth. I also thought, *How will they ever come to a knowledge of the truth if God's people don't go to them in love?*

I still believed it was important to change sex education, but I was determined to go about it differently. Immediately, I stopped my angry speeches at public meetings and took another approach. I called the executive director of the Colorado organization that trains teachers for Comprehensive Health Education (which includes sex education) and asked her if she would be willing to meet with me to dialogue. I explained that my purpose was simply to see if we could find some common ground and learn where we disagreed. Although I didn't deserve it after all I had done, she agreed to meet with me.

Over the following year, we spent approximately twenty hours in dialogue. We *did* find common ground. We both wanted healthier young people and a better society. Although in many ways we continued to disagree, she was willing to make significant revisions to the curriculum her organization had published. They even added a chapter acknowledging that abstinence is a wise and desirable choice for young people.

In the process, this public servant and I built a friendship and mutual respect for one another. After only the second time we had met, God confirmed the need for dialogue in the Spirit of Christ when she said to me, "I want you to know that in all the years I've been doing this, this is the first time I have been able to sit down with someone who has an opposing view and have honest communication." This woman had been working with the public for twenty-two years.

This experience changed my life. Since 1990, I had been running Accountability Ministries as a marriage reconciliation ministry. But now I reengineered it to focus on teaching others how to follow the principles God taught me through hard experience and biblical study. The fact that I had worked in the area of sex education was incidental; building bridges is a skill useful in every kind of interpersonal relationship. The vision I see is God's people replacing gossip, quarreling, and stereotyping with dialogue in the Spirit of Christ, beginning in our homes and churches and then spreading into all of society to draw people to Jesus Christ for God's glory.

Building bridges, not walls, is about:

- *Communicating in ways that bear fruit for God's glory.* Relationships, instead of issues, must be our priority. As we work at having respectful, honest relationships with those who have different viewpoints, we will be able to really talk about the matters that concern us.
- *Learning to become servants of God.* We are not to be lone warriors, fighting for a cause because it matters to *us.* We are, instead, to remain firmly under the orders of our Commander-in-Chief, and He is always concerned that people come to a greater knowledge of the truth and of Himself.
- *Living transformed lives.* Knowing what's right is not the most important thing. What's most important is God working in our hearts through His Holy Spirit to bring about needed changes in our lives so that we become the kind of people who can make a difference in others' lives.
- *Maturing in Christ by becoming other-minded rather than self-centered.* A part of growing up into the likeness of Christ is replacing conditional love with unconditional

love even toward the undeserving and unthankful. It is also making time for, and being available to dialogue with, people who disagree with us.

- *Remembering, above all else, our desperate need for Jesus Christ.* Apart from Christ, we are incapable of loving each other as Christ has loved us and responding as He would to people with opposing views. Our need for Christ-centered grace never goes away.

As you can see, my vision for bridge building is less about *learning what to do* than it is about *becoming who you should be.* I hope you're prepared for a course that challenges your view of yourself! I encourage you to embrace the challenge and trust in God to work in you for the best.

And remember, this vision is really not new with me. It was new two thousand years ago when Jesus first established the defining characteristic of His people. "A new command I give you: Love one another. As I have loved you, so you must love one another. By this all men will know that you are my disciples, if you love one another" (John 13:34-35). Building bridges is basically about love.

Out of love, Christ built a bridge from earth to heaven for us. Let us, likewise out of love, build bridges of understanding with others.

WHAT TO EXPECT FROM THIS BOOK

My friend, I honor you for your willingness to pursue this course in building bridges. I really do! Most people prefer to grumble about the problems they see but do nothing about them, or else they choose to angrily proclaim their views regardless of how they are perceived by others. But you're not willing to give up either truth *or* love, and you're ready to lay out the effort it takes to learn how to dialogue in the Spirit of Christ. You're the type of person the Lord will use to change the world.

Right now I'd like to tell you what you can expect from this book as soon as you move beyond the introduction. The first thing you need to know is there are twelve separate *Building Bridges* studies lying ahead of you. Each one will most likely take from thirty to sixty minutes, depending on how you approach them. You can do several studies in a row, one right after the other, or you can spread them out, perhaps one a week.

I have carefully designed these studies so that they may be used by individuals or by groups. The material is self-explanatory, so if you're disciplined, you can work through the book successfully on your own. But I recommend that, if possible, you do the studies with one or more other persons. These studies are great in church adult education classes, parachurch training programs, or other groups. You can get the most out of the experience by talking over the issues with friends and by holding each other accountable. The appendix contains general guidelines for the study group leader.

The materials needed for this course are very basic. Each participant will need a copy of this book, a pen or pencil, and a Bible—that's all! This book quotes from the New International Version (NIV) of the Bible, so it might be best if you use an NIV, though that's not a requirement. And as this is an interactive study, you should feel free to mark up the book as much as you like. Personalize it; make it your own.

Meanwhile, the format of the studies is simple and easy to follow. On the first page of each study you will find introductory material to let you know where you'll be going in the study. Then the body of each *Building Bridges* study has two major sections: Bible study and personal application. In the Bible study section you will be interacting with one or more relevant Bible passages to discover God's wisdom on the subject. Then you will move on to questions and other material that will challenge you to evaluate yourself and put into practice what you learned in the Bible study.

Scattered throughout a *Building Bridges* study are certain special features. Please note these:

Big Idea—The central concept around which the entire study is wrapped.

Bible Basis—A verse listing that serves as a heads-up to the main passages you'll be focusing upon in the study.

Notes, Quotes, & Anecdotes—A story or excerpt that sheds light upon the subject in a different way.

Meditation Verse—A Bible verse, relevant to the topic at hand, that is suitable for meditation and prayer.

Group Activity—An optional activity that you can use if you are studying this
course with others.

My Commitment—Space where you can record one or more action steps you
believe God wants you to take in response to the study.

Big Idea Review—A repetition of the central concept at the end of the
study—just to make sure you don't miss it!

Bridge to God—A prayer that you can use verbatim or as a model for your
own prayer to wrap up your study time.

Coming Up—A quickie preview of what to expect in the following *Building
Bridges* study.

And now all that remains is to get started! A desire to be able to dialogue more
wholesomely with others, combined with an openness to what God wants to teach you,
can make *Building Bridges* a turning point in your life. I pray it may be so.

THREE-WAY CONVERSATION

BIG IDEA: Dialogue with another person will be honoring to God only if we involve Christ in it.

BIBLE BASIS: I Samuel 17:32-34,36-37,40,45-47,50; John 15:5-8

Many a Christian has been surprised and disappointed by the negative outcome of a dialogue he was engaged in. A common denominator in almost all those cases is that the Christian tried to interact with the other person *on his own,* that is, without involving Christ in the situation.

In one sense, of course, Christ is with us all the time, no matter what we do. But it is certainly possible for a Christian to rely on her own resources in a dialogue rather than praying for Christ's guidance and keeping in mind Christ's teachings in the Bible. And that's the road that leads to disaster.

A favorite memory verse for many is Proverbs 3:5: "Trust in the LORD with all your heart and lean not on your own understanding." That verse reminds us that our knowledge is as a drop compared to the sea of God's wisdom, and it is silly for us to sip the drop rather than drink deeply from the sea. This is true most particularly in the tricky interactions we have with other people.

In this *Building Bridges* study, we will look at a boy who knew better than his elders that "the battle is the LORD's" and at an analogy of Jesus' that helps us comprehend what it means to remain connected with Him. This Bible basis will show us how to make Jesus the invisible participant in a three-way conversation.

BIBLE STUDY

POWER WITH GOD

I could have chosen any number of Bible passages that illustrate how we have power when we ally ourselves with God and how we are helpless without Him. But two will suffice. As you study these passages, think about the way your dialogues have gone better when you have consciously tried to engage the other person in the power and Spirit of the Lord.

GOD AND ONE SMOOTH STONE

Picture this: The Israelite army is on one hill; the Philistine army is on another. Every day a gigantic soldier from the Philistine army, Goliath, taunts the Israelites, urging them to send someone to fight him in one-on-one combat. No one dares, and the Israelites daily become more disheartened. Then a shepherd boy approaches Saul, the Israelite king, for permission to fight Goliath.

1 Samuel 17:32-34,36-37,40,45-47,50:

> David said to Saul, "Let no one lose heart on account of this Philistine; your servant will go and fight him."
>
> Saul replied, "You are not able to go out against this Philistine and fight him; you are only a boy, and he has been a fighting man from his youth."
>
> But David said to Saul, . . . "Your servant has killed both the lion and the

bear; this uncircumcised Philistine will be like one of them, because he has defied the armies of the living God. The LORD who delivered me from the paw of the lion and the paw of the bear will deliver me from the hand of this Philistine."

Saul said to David, "Go, and the LORD be with you." . . .

[David] took his staff in his hand, chose five smooth stones from the stream, put them in the pouch of his shepherd's bag and, with his sling in his hand, approached the Philistine. . . .

David said to the Philistine, "You come against me with sword and spear and javelin, but I come against you in the name of the LORD Almighty, the God of the armies of Israel, whom you have defied. This day the LORD will hand you over to me, and I'll strike you down and cut off your head. . . . All those gathered here will know that it is not by sword or spear that the LORD saves; for the battle is the LORD's, and he will give all of you into our hands." . . .

So David triumphed over the Philistine with a sling and a stone; without a sword in his hand he struck down the Philistine and killed him.

What words would you use to describe the Israelite army before David defeated Goliath?

What words would you use to describe David's attitude?

What reasons did David have for trusting God?

What resources did David have for his contest with Goliath?

What did David accomplish, and why was he successful?

A FRUIT-BEARING BRANCH

Before leaving His disciples to return to heaven, Jesus instructed them on how they could be successful in their spiritual endeavors. For this, the Lord used an analogy that would have been readily understood in a wine-producing country like Israel.

John 15:5-8:

> "I am the vine; you are the branches. If a man remains in me and I in him, he will bear much fruit; apart from me you can do nothing. If anyone does not remain in me, he is like a branch that is thrown away and withers; such branches are picked up, thrown into the fire and burned. If you remain in me and my words remain in you, ask whatever you wish, and it will be given you. This is to my Father's glory, that you bear much fruit, showing yourselves to be my disciples."

In Jesus' teaching, what is the vine? What are the branches? What is the fruit?

What happens when a branch does not remain connected to the vine?

What happens when a branch *does* remain connected to the vine?

Practically speaking, what does it mean to "remain in" Christ and His words? (Hint: Check out 1 John 2:24 and 3:11.)

Label the vine below with the name "Jesus." Label the branch on the vine with your own name. Label the grapes with the kinds of spiritual fruit you would like to bear as a result of abiding in Christ.

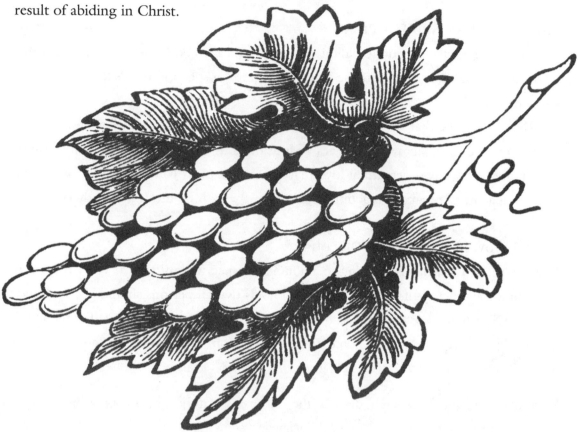

Throughout history, God's followers have known effectiveness beyond their own resources when they have sought to act on God's behalf and with His help. And since the advent of Christ, people who have been connected with the Lord through faith and the Spirit have enjoyed a God-given ability to bear spiritual fruit. This connection is what we need when we engage others in dialogue about issues that matter to us.

▶ MEDITATION VERSE

Do not be terrified; do not be discouraged, for the LORD your God will be with you wherever you go.

—JOSHUA 1:9

PERSONAL APPLICATION

THE THIRD MAN AND HIS PLAN

As stated in the introduction, building bridges is basically about love. When we involve Christ in our dialogues, we converse with the purpose of showing God's love to our dialogue partner.

This is not love that we "work up" on our own. In fact, we might have few natural reasons to love someone who disagrees with us on an important matter. The love we're talking about here is supernatural love that we receive from Christ and pass on to our dialogue partner. It makes a real difference in how we communicate with others.

CASE STUDY: A EUTHANASIA DIALOGUE

Imagine that a Christian is speaking to a nonChristian about euthanasia. The Christian is defending the sanctity-of-life position, which holds that all persons should be protected. The nonChristian is defending the quality-of-life position, holding that if someone is severely ill or otherwise dysfunctional, there is no reason why that person can't be put to death. The conversation starts to get intense.

What words do you think might describe the Christian's attitude if he is approaching this dialogue without Christ (fearful, prideful, inclined to stereotype)?

What words do you think might describe the Christian's attitude if he had prayed for Christ's help and never lost track of the primacy of love (servant, honest, hopeful)?

What would the Christian's priorities in this dialogue be if he is involving Christ in it?

What do you think the nonChristian's reaction might be as she notes the Christian's loving attitude?

YOU AND CHRIST

Can you think of a time when you engaged someone in dialogue "on your own," that is, without seeking to involve Christ in it? Describe what happened.

Has there been another time when you effectively involved the "third man," Jesus Christ, in your dialogue, thus turning it into a three-way conversation? Describe what happened that time.

What actions could you take to cultivate your relationship with Christ?

Which of Christ's teachings do you think is wise to have fresh in one's mind while approaching a dialogue with another?

How might a current dialogue of yours be different if you were to focus on involving Christ and showing love?

NOTES, QUOTES, & ANECDOTES

A Window to His Glory

Bring the glory of Christ with you as you minister. He is your only hope of change. Confront one another not just with human words, human wisdom, and human arguments. Confront one another with the presence and glory of Christ. Reinforce the reality that he is here and active. Be a window to his glory!

This means letting go of any hope that *we* can produce change. You and I *don't* produce change in others; it is always the result of God's power and grace at work. So we let go of human demands. We don't try to impress people with how much we've experienced. We don't try to force change by manipulation. We don't seek to get results with a loud voice or inflammatory words. We won't bribe, bargain, or make deals. We won't seek to get responses by guilt, condemnation, or judgment. We don't trust in our airtight arguments. We recognize that if these things could bring lasting change to the human heart, Christ would never have come to suffer and die. The most important encounter in personal ministry is not people's encounter with us, but their encounter with him. We are simply called to set up that encounter.

—PAUL DAVID TRIPP

In the space below, write a prayer that you could use to invite Christ's presence and participation in a dialogue with another person.

GROUP ACTIVITY (OPTIONAL)

If you are studying the *Building Bridges* course with others, get together with one other person. First, share about current dialogues you are involved in. Then pray for each other, asking Christ to be present in each other's lives in a powerful way, guiding and blessing as you dialogue further, with the goal of bringing glory to God.

MY COMMITMENT:

BIG IDEA REVIEW

Our dialogue with another person will be honoring to God only if we involve Christ in it.

BRIDGE TO GOD

Lord, I see now how I have too often approached a conversation without seeking to involve You in it. I have relied on my own all-too-inadequate resources, and the dialogue process has suffered as a result. Forgive me for this mistake and help me in the future to always seek to engage others in Your power and love. In Christ's name, amen.

COMING UP

Get ready for the still more challenging subject of surrendering one's goals for a dialogue and accepting in their place God's goals. He might be wanting to do something different in one of your relationships—something that has never occurred to you!

SURRENDERING THE OUTCOME TO GOD

BIG IDEA: When we surrender to the will of God, He will accomplish His goals in
our difficult relationships.

BIBLE BASIS: Daniel 3 and 6 (selected verses); Luke 22:41-44

See if this has ever described you: You were facing a tense situation with another person, so you constructed a strategy to "defeat" the other person; you let your feelings of outrage and superiority bubble up to give you strength; and then you charged into the battle. If you thought about God at all, it was only to pause a moment and ask Him to bless your prearranged plan.

If that has never described you, then I can tell you it *has* described me—and probably many others as well. All too often we go to God last (if ever) in our crafty maneuverings when we find ourselves at odds with someone.

What if we were to take another approach? What if we were to forget our own will and seek God's will instead?

Surrendering our will to the Father is a key to building bridges. But surrender in this case, paradoxically, leads not to defeat but to victory. When we surrender to God, we let go of the outcome we want and invite God to use us for His purposes—and He does! Scripture shows us that when we give in to God, the results are always far above anything that our merely human minds could have conceived.

In this *Building Bridges* study, we will be taking a whirlwind trip through two stories in the book of Daniel as well as observing our Lord at His most vulnerable moment. All this for the purpose of learning the critical importance of seeking God's will and not our own as we dialogue with others.

BIBLE STUDY

GOING GOD'S WAY

Many of God's servants throughout history, when at their best, have held firmly to God's way in the face of intense pressure to turn aside. We can learn from, and take courage from, their examples. And yet no one provides a greater example of obedience to God than Christ our Lord.

FOUR FAITHFUL FRIENDS

In one of Israel's darkest hours, the nation was taken over by the Babylonians and many of its young aristocrats were hauled back to Babylon to serve the Babylonian king. Among these young Jews were four friends named Daniel, Shadrach, Meshach, and Abednego. All four were devout followers of the one true God. They would find their faith tested in the pagan environment where they were transplanted.

For Shadrach, Meshach, and Abednego, the test came soon. The Babylonian king, Nebuchadnezzar, set up a huge gold statue and required all his officials to bow down to it. Shadrach, Meshach, and Abednego refused to do so, since it would violate their commitment to God, and as a result they were cast into a furnace to be burned. An odd thing happened, though: They were unharmed by the fierce fire and were kept company by a mysterious fourth figure (an angel or perhaps God Himself). Nebuchadnezzar realized he had done wrong and rescued the three men. You can read this story in Daniel 3.

Many years later, Daniel faced a similar challenge. He had by this time reached a high position in the government of Darius the Mede and was poised to occupy an even higher position. Some jealous bureaucrats set a trap for him by having the king declare a month-long period during which only the king could be worshiped. Daniel went right on praying to the true God, and so the king reluctantly had him thrown into a pit filled with hungry lions. What happened? The lions acted like tame kittens and left Daniel alone! The next day, therefore, the king had Daniel removed from the pit and restored him to favor. This story is told in Daniel 6.

These two stories of faith testing offer some remarkable parallels:

The four men put their trust in God.

> Praise be to the God of Shadrach, Meshach, and Abednego. . . . They trusted in him.
>
> —Daniel 3:28

> When Daniel was lifted from the den, no wound was found on him, because he had trusted in his God.
>
> —Daniel 6:23

God was with them.

> Look! I see four men walking around in the fire, unbound and unharmed, and the fourth looks like a son of the gods.
>
> —Daniel 3:25

> My God sent his angel, and he shut the mouths of the lions.
>
> —Daniel 6:22

God delivered them from their enemies.

> If we are thrown into the blazing furnace, the God we serve is able to save us from it, and he will rescue us from your hand, O king.

> —DANIEL 3:17

> May your God, whom you serve continually, rescue you!

> —DANIEL 6:16

God was exalted, even by the ungodly.

> Then Nebuchadnezzar said, "Praise be to the God of Shadrach, Meshach and Abednego. . . . No other god can save in this way."

> —DANIEL 3:28-29

> I [King Darius] issue a decree that in every part of my kingdom people must fear and reverence the God of Daniel. "For he is the living God and he endures forever."

> —DANIEL 6:26

God's servants enjoyed success and prospered.

> The king promoted Shadrach, Meshach and Abednego in the province of Babylon.

> —DANIEL 3:30

> Daniel prospered during the reign of Darius and the reign of Cyrus the Persian.

> —DANIEL 6:28

What pressures were placed on Daniel, Shadrach, Meshach, and Abednego to conform to their society?

What excuses might the four men have been tempted to make for bending to pressure?

What do you think kept them faithful to the Lord?

What did surrendering to God's will mean for Shadrach, Meshach, and Abednego? What did it mean for Daniel?

What were the outcomes of their surrender for themselves? For others?

A LAMB TO THE SLAUGHTER

Years before Jesus lived on the earth, the prophet Isaiah portrayed the Messiah as being "led like a lamb to the slaughter" (Isaiah 53:7). Yet as we look in on Jesus in the Garden of Gethsemane, we realize that, just like us, He struggled with surrendering to the will of the Father.

Luke 22:41-44:

> [Jesus] knelt down and prayed, "Father, if you are willing, take this cup from me; yet not my will, but yours be done." An angel from heaven appeared to him and strengthened him. And being in anguish, he prayed more earnestly, and his sweat was like drops of blood falling to the ground.

What was the bitter "cup" that Jesus so desperately wished He did not have to drink?

How did the Father show His compassion for His suffering Son?

> → ◄
> ## NOTES, QUOTES, & ANECDOTES
>
> ### The Power of Lamblikeness
>
> We may well ask what gives the Blood its power! . . . Not the Blood of the Warrior, but the Blood of *the Lamb!* In other words, that which gives the precious Blood its power with God for men is the lamb-like disposition of the One who shed it. . . .
>
> But the title "the Lamb" has a deeper meaning. It describes His character. He is the Lamb in that He is meek and lowly in heart, gentle and unresisting, and all the time surrendering His own will to the Father's for the blessing and saving of men. Anyone but the Lamb would have resented and resisted the treatment men gave Him. But He, in obedience to the Father and out of love for us, did neither. Men did what they liked to Him and for our sakes He yielded all the time. When He was reviled, He reviled not again. When He suffered, He threatened not. No standing up for His rights, no hitting back, no resentment, no complaining! How different from us! . . . The nailing and the lifting up, the piercing of His side and the flowing of His Blood—none of these things would ever have been, had He not been the Lamb. And all that to pay the price of *my* sin! So we see He is not merely the Lamb because He died on the Cross, but He died upon the Cross because He is the Lamb.
>
> Let us ever see this disposition in the Blood. Let every mention of the Blood call to mind the deep humility and self-surrender of the Lamb, for it is this disposition that gives the Blood its wonderful power with God. . . . Humility, lamb-likeness, the surrender of our wills to God, are what He looks for supremely from man.
>
> —ROY HESSION

How did Jesus react to the anguish He felt inside?

Judging by what you know of the events that followed Jesus' prayer in the Garden of Gethsemane, what was the outcome of His anguished struggle in prayer? (Hint: Check out Hebrews 5:7.)

Circle or highlight the words "not my will, but yours be done" in the previous Scripture quote (page 29). These words encapsulate a principle that can serve us well in all our decisions and relationships. One theologian says he repeats to himself the words "Not mine, thine; not mine, thine" whenever he is tempted to try to control events. You might like to try the same exercise.

▶ MEDITATION VERSE

"Not by might nor by power, but by my Spirit," says the LORD Almighty.

—ZECHARIAH 4:6

PERSONAL APPLICATION

NOT MY WILL, BUT HIS

Sometimes surrendering to the will of God is harder than at other times. One difficult time is when we are engaged in a dialogue with someone who is defending a position that we just can't stand. Our blood is up and every instinct within us urges us to attack, attack, attack! And that's when we're supposed to *love* the other person and put that person's *well-being* before our desire to change his or her mind?

Yes, I'm afraid so. This doesn't mean we can't continue to promote the truth (more on that in future *Building Bridges* studies), but we have to be sensitive to what God might want to do in the relationship. He is always wanting to draw people nearer to Himself. If you attack, attack, attack, you may drive the other person not only further from yourself but also from God.

Surrender and let God win.

CONTROL FREAK?

In general, how prone are you to trying to control the events in your life? Circle a number below, 1 meaning "not much of a controller" and 10 meaning "major control freak."

1   2   3   4   5   6   7   8   9   10

What messages from society may influence your desire for control?

What inner motives do you think may lie behind your desire to control the outcome of a dialogue?

Think back to a conflict situation when you neglected to consider what God's will might be. What was the situation, and what was the outcome?

GOD CAN HANDLE IT

Is the idea of surrendering your will to God's scary to you? If so, why?

What kinds of attitudinal changes does one have to make in order to surrender one's own will and accept God's?

How does one discover what God's will *is* so that one can surrender to it?

What biblical principles (reflecting God's will) apply generally to a Christian who is in dialogue with another person? (Hint: Check out 2 Timothy 2:24-26.)

Think of an interpersonal conflict that you are currently involved in. What is your will in the matter? What do you think God's will for it might be?

What specific changes do you have to make to begin pursuing God's will instead of your own?

GROUP ACTIVITY (OPTIONAL)

If you are studying the *Building Bridges* course with a group, get together with two or three other group members. Discuss the following list of scenarios, suggesting what the objectives of the people involved might be, contrasting them with the possible objectives of God.

- A Christian woman who had an abortion and repented of it is talking with a nonChristian teenage neighbor who is pregnant and unmarried.
- A Christian husband and wife are arguing about the distribution of household chores.
- Two church leaders are discussing whether more money should be devoted to missions or to their church's building program.
- A brand-new Christian who works in a small business owned by another Christian is raising the issue of the owner's questionable business ethics.
- A Christian is speaking at a citizens' forum on the pending issue of legalizing gambling in the city.

MY COMMITMENT:

BIG IDEA REVIEW

When we surrender to the will of God, He will accomplish His goals in our difficult relationships.

BRIDGE TO GOD

Almighty God, I confess that I have often pursued my own course without a thought of You. Forgive me for this and make me sensitive to my need of seeking Your desires for me. What You want is always best. I humbly submit to Your will for all my relationships, present and future. In Christ's name, amen.

COMING UP

The themes of this study are extended in the next one as we look at the choices we have to make between the world's approach to dialogue and Christ's approach.

WORLDLINESS VERSUS CHRISTLIKENESS

BIG IDEA: We can build bridges only when we cease being conformed to the world and instead seek to respond to others as Christ would.

BIBLE BASIS: Luke 10:30-35; Philippians 2:3-8; James 4:1-3; 1 John 2:15; 3:16

Paul Tripp, in *War of Words,* says, "God is at work, taking people who instinctively speak for themselves and transforming them into people who effectively speak for Him."

If we view conflict from God's perspective, we will recognize it as an opportunity to mature in Christ and respond as Christ would to people who have opposing views. Our highest objective in conflict should be to respond in ways that glorify God, rather than to win an argument and persuade someone to our point of view. Our biggest obstacle is the ease with which we fall into the ways of the world (that is, the sinful patterns of human society).

On the following pages we will look at biblical principles and personal applications that help us understand the difference between responding in a selfish, worldly way and responding as Christ would to people with opposing views.

BIBLE STUDY

A CLEAR CONTRAST

In this Bible study section we will look at three pairs of scriptural passages that present contrasts. Each pair is different, and yet each gets at the fundamental conflict between worldliness and Christlikeness.

SELF-CENTERED OR OTHER-MINDED?

Two New Testament passages present the options that lie before us as we engage others in dialogue. In one the apostle James criticized some of the early Christians for their self-ishness, which led to quarreling. In the other the apostle Paul described the need for Christians to adopt Christlike humility.

James 4:1-3:

> What causes fights and quarrels among you? Don't they come from your desires that battle within you? You want something but don't get it. You kill and covet, but you cannot have what you want. You quarrel and fight. You do not have, because you do not ask God. When you ask, you do not receive, because you ask with wrong motives, that you may spend what you get on your pleasures.

Philippians 2:3-8:

> Do nothing out of selfish ambition or vain conceit, but in humility consider others better than yourselves. Each of you should look not only to your own interests, but also to the interests of others.
>
> > Your attitude should be the same as that of Christ Jesus:
> >
> > Who, being in very nature God,
> >
> > did not consider equality with God something to be grasped,
> >
> > but made himself nothing,
> >
> > taking the very nature of a servant,
> >
> > being made in human likeness.

And being found in appearance as a man,
he humbled himself
and became obedient to death—even death on a cross!

In the churches to which James wrote, what were some of the things going on in the hearts of the believers?

What kinds of things were the believers doing as a result of their desires?

How did the Christians' selfishness affect their prayers?

In contrast, what attitudes did Paul encourage in his readers?

In what ways did Jesus model humility for us?

CONDITIONAL LOVE OR UNCONDITIONAL?

Christians have always been tempted to split their devotion between God and certain things of this world. The apostle John warned about love of the world. He also reminded us that unconditional love requires the laying down of our self-centered lives and the surrendering of our rights out of love for God and others.

1 John 2:15:

Do not love the world or anything in the world. If anyone loves the world, the love of the Father is not in him.

NOTES, QUOTES, & ANECDOTES

Pursuing Love

A pastor in Aurora, Colorado, shared a story with me regarding a marital conflict in his church and how the church leadership intervened with church discipline as outlined in Matthew 18:15-17. The process took a surprising twist.

As the wife was shown her fault in the matter, she was quick to repent. However, the husband was not. So the elders took one or two others along to establish the facts.

The husband remained unwilling to listen, so they told the story to the entire congregation. Afterward, the unrepentant husband responded, "I don't care what you say. I'm going to divorce my wife and I will leave the fellowship."

Soon after, the man divorced his wife, left the fellowship, and moved to California. But that wasn't the end of the story.

One of the elders, who had been involved in the church discipline, cared enough about this brother in Christ that at his own expense he flew to California to talk to him. Through that act of kindness, the previously unrepentant brother broke down and wept. He became vulnerable, shared his weaknesses, and explained why he was hurting so much, and why he had behaved so poorly. The man repented, moved back to Colorado, remarried his wife, and was restored to the fellowship.

This kind of thing could happen a lot more—*if we weren't too busy!*

—JEFF ROSENAU

1 John 3:16:

This is how we know what love is: Jesus Christ laid down his life for us. And we ought to lay down our lives for our brothers.

Why do you think love of the world is incompatible with love of God?

What is the difference between the way the world responds to being wronged and Christ's response to being wronged?

Why does worldliness prompt a person to extend love to another only so long as that person can expect to get something in return?

TOO BUSY OR AVAILABLE?

Jesus told a famous story in which different characters exemplify different responses to a need. The priest and Levite were religious leaders, belonging to the same ethnic group and religion as the injured man.

The Samaritan, on the other hand, was a member of a religious group that was hated by the Jews.

Luke 10:30-32:

> "A man was going down from Jerusalem to Jericho, when he fell into the hands of robbers. They stripped him of his clothes, beat him and went away, leaving him half dead. A priest happened to be going down the same road, and when he saw the man, he passed by on the other side. So too, a Levite, when he came to the place and saw him, passed by on the other side."

Luke 10:33-35:

> "But a Samaritan, as he traveled, came where the man was; and when he saw him, he took pity on him. He went to him and bandaged his wounds, pouring on oil and wine. Then he put the man on his own donkey, took him to an inn and took care of him. The next day he took out two silver coins and gave them to the innkeeper, 'Look after him,' he said, 'and when I return, I will reimburse you for any extra expense you may have.'"

Why might we have expected the priest and Levite to help the injured man?

What excuses might the two religious leaders have used to justify in their own minds their passing by the injured man?

Why might we have expected the Samaritan to ignore the injured Jew?

What lesson can we draw from the fact that the Samaritan not only helped the injured man but helped as thoroughly as he could?

What lesson about priorities and the use of one's time can we draw from this parable?

In your Bible, check out the story that (not coincidentally) follows this one—the story of Mary and Martha (see Luke 10:38-42). What does this story add to our picture of the importance of making time for God and others?

Below is a chart summarizing what we can learn about dialogue from the three pairs of Bible passages:

WORLDLINESS	CHRISTLIKENESS
James 4:1-3 Worldly people are *self-centered*. They respond by fighting and quarreling when they don't get their way, causing disunity.	**Philippians 2:3-8** Christlike people are *other-minded*. They are more concerned about others' interests than their own, and this can produce peace and unity.
1 John 2:15 Worldly people offer *conditional love*. That is, they give their love when doing so serves their self-interest and they withdraw their love when it doesn't.	**1 John 3:16** Christlike people respond with *unconditional love* even to the undeserving and unthankful. After all, this is what Christ has done with us.
Luke 10:30-32,40 Worldly people are *too busy* to build meaningful relationships with God and other people. They have different priorities.	**Luke 10:33-35,39** Christlike people make themselves *available* to other people. They place their highest priority on building meaningful relationships with God and people.

▶ MEDITATION VERSE

Brothers, I could not address you as spiritual but as worldly—mere infants in
Christ. I gave you milk, not solid food, for you were not yet ready for it. Indeed,
you are still not ready. You are still worldly. For since there is jealousy and quarreling among you, are you not worldly? Are you not acting like mere men?

—1 CORINTHIANS 3:1-3

PERSONAL APPLICATION

CHRISTLIKE DIALOGUE

Christlike behavior is something we can learn as we deliberately reject the world's messages (which reinforce our own natural selfishness) and focus instead on our great role
model, Jesus Christ. All this has many practical implications for our dialogues with others. As we are other-minded, unconditionally loving, and available, we will engage others in ways that please our God.

CASE STUDY: HILLSIDE AND HYMNS

Hillside Church is an older congregation with a rich history of evangelism and service to
the community. Lately, the new worship leader has experimented by mixing contemporary praise choruses in with the usual diet of hymns and anthems. This has gotten more
than a few members talking. One church elder, Dave, decided to share his concerns with
the worship leader, Ashley, after church.

"Do you have a minute, Ashley?" asked Dave. "I'd like to talk to you about these
new songs you've been introducing."

"Well, a bunch of us are going out to lunch," replied Ashley.

"Won't take long," Dave assured her.

"Yeah, okay," said Ashley. She stopped to listen, but her body language expressed her
impatience.

"It's about this new music you've been introducing. Have you really thought about it? I mean, I don't get anything out of it, and I know I'm not alone in that. It seems to me it's more like entertainment or performance; it's not real worship. Hymns—now, they are dignified and show respect for God. And another thing . . . "

"Yeah, thanks for sharing. They're waiting for me. Bye," said Ashley, running off.

Both felt dissatisfied with the conversation.

How did time issues impact this first meeting between the two?

Ashley called Dave later in the week and apologized for being so rushed when they talked earlier. She invited him to stop by the church and talk some more before choir rehearsal.

What she didn't say was that she had in the meantime remembered he was an elder in the church. She was worried that her paid position as worship leader might be in jeopardy if she couldn't soothe Dave's mind about the contemporary songs.

At their second meeting, Ashley was extremely polite and attentive to Dave. Dave, of course, was pleased by this.

As Dave reiterated his point that hymns are proven aids to worship, Ashley nodded and smiled. She never came out and said she would stop leading praise choruses, but she kept agreeing with Dave about how great hymns are and how she intended to keep using them. Dave was still more pleased.

At the end of their meeting, Ashley said, "Well, I've got to go to rehearsal. I guess you're going to the elders meeting."

"Not really. My term just ended," explained Dave.

Ashley's face fell as she thought of all the effort she had wasted being nice to someone who was not in a position to affect her job after all. Dave noticed her change of expression and wondered.

How did conditional love interfere with genuine communication at this second meeting?

Several weeks passed, and Ashley kept avoiding Dave. The truth was, she was feeling guilty about never really engaging him on the question that interested him. And she felt that she had, in a way, been trying to use him.

Finally, she got up the courage to talk to him after Sunday school and apologize for her treatment of him. She thought he would hate her, but actually he was relieved and friendly after her apology. He had been feeling that something was fishy, especially as Ashley had not altered her mix of music in the services.

Dave invited Ashley to have dinner with him and his wife that evening. At this third meeting Ashley gave her honest reason for liking contemporary music.

"This church has always been concerned about reaching out to the unsaved," said Ashley. "Most hymns were written generations ago. They don't sound anything like the music that most unsaved people listen to these days. So if nonChristians come to our service and hear only the old-time music, the experience is going to seem really alien to them. They wouldn't connect with worship at all. If we're serious about evangelism, we've got to make our service a place that's friendly for people who are trying to find out about Jesus."

Dave said he'd never thought of it that way. He admitted that he had probably been opposed to the contemporary music because he, personally, was more comfortable with hymns. He said he appreciated Ashley's sensitivity to evangelism. She said she appreciated his flexibility.

As they continued to talk, they agreed to keep monitoring the balance of music so that the long-term members could worship with music they felt comfortable with while also making Hillside's services into experiences where unbelievers could discover God.

How did being other-minded result in a positive outcome for Ashley and Dave's relationship and for their dialogue?

CHRISTLIKENESS SELF-EVALUATION

What makes it hard for you to put aside your selfish interests and focus on the needs of others?

Thinking of a dialogue in which you are currently involved, what would you say is some way that you could be other-minded and serve your dialogue partner?

Has anybody ever extended to you their love only as long as they thought they could get something out of you, then withdrawn it? How did that feel?

How can having an undivided love for God enable you to show unconditional love to the people with whom you are in dialogue?

What are some of the priorities that you are tempted to believe are more important than building meaningful relationships with God and people?

What changes can you make to become more available to the people God has and will bring into your life?

Our Father is calling us to return to Him, to repent of our conformity to this world, and to mature in Christ so that we can bear fruit for His glory. Are we willing to do so? As brothers and sisters in Christ, do we love God enough to encourage loving relationships and hold each other accountable to replace gossip and quarreling with one-to-one dialogue in the Spirit of Christ so the world will know we are Christ's disciples by our love for one another?

GROUP ACTIVITY (OPTIONAL)

If you are studying *Building Bridges* in a group, get together with one other person and role-play a dialogue in two different ways. The first way is one in which both partners are being worldly (self-centered, conditionally loving, too busy). The second way is one in which both are being Christlike (other-minded, unconditionally loving, available).

Pick any subject you like. Remember that great argumentation is not the purpose; practicing the two approaches is the purpose.

MY COMMITMENT:

BIG IDEA REVIEW

We can build bridges only when we cease being conformed to the world and instead seek to respond to others as Christ would.

BRIDGE TO GOD

Dear Lord, I love the Son whom You sent and I want to be like Him. Help me as I seek to treat others with the same sort of love with which He treated those whom He met by the roads of Israel. Help me root out the vestiges of worldliness inside me and render myself wholly over to You. In Christ's name, amen.

COMING UP

In Building Bridges *study four we continue looking at contrasts between dialoguing our way and dialoguing God's way. There lies a choice before us. Which way will we go?*

THE CHOICE TO OBEY

BIG IDEA: Having a dialogue that builds bridges means making a choice to do it God's way instead of one's own.

BIBLE BASIS: Galatians 5:16-25; James 3:13-18

So, you think you know how to carry on a dialogue with someone? Where do you get your ideas about dialoguing? Have you thought about that?

Before launching into a dialogue that could have great consequences for good or for ill, it is best to reconsider your principles for dialogue. If they aren't trustworthy, it's high time to throw them out and start with new ones.

Too often our ideas about dialogue have (at least partly) come from untrustworthy sources. We have picked up worldly concepts that will not serve us well. We need a reorientation of our heads around godly truth.

And that's not easy. The world, the flesh, and the Devil are all clamoring to get us to think their way. We have to make a conscious choice to shut them out and instead listen to the still, small voice of God's Spirit. It's a matter of Christian obedience.

In *Building Bridges* study four we look at some Bible passages that present a stark contrast between the world's way and God's way. The choice is clear—but will we make the right choice for our dialogues?

BIBLE STUDY

THE SPIRITUAL AND SINFUL OPTIONS

If we were to listen to the world, we would think traditional categories of morality are not really of much importance. But if we pay attention to Scripture, we see that behavior is very important indeed, for it reflects our obedience to God. The following two passages will serve as examples for us, with an emphasis on those moral qualities that have an impact on our dialogue.

THE TASTIEST FRUIT

The apostle Paul often had to remind the new believers in his care that holiness does not come naturally. It comes from making choices to follow the dictates of the Holy Spirit, not the dictates of the sinful nature that lives on in us even after we have become Christians. The consequences of these choices are played out in our relationships with others.

Galatians 5:16-25:

> Live by the Spirit, and you will not gratify the desires of the sinful nature. For the sinful nature desires what is contrary to the Spirit, and the Spirit what is contrary to the sinful nature. They are in conflict with each other, so that you do not do what you want. . . .
>
> The acts of the sinful nature are obvious: sexual immorality, impurity and debauchery; idolatry and witchcraft; hatred, discord, jealousy, fits of rage, selfish ambition, dissensions, factions and envy; drunkenness, orgies, and the like. I warn you, as I did before, that those who live like this will not inherit the kingdom of God.

But the fruit of the Spirit is love, joy, peace, patience, kindness, goodness, faithfulness, gentleness and self-control. Against such things there is no law. Those who belong to Christ Jesus have crucified the sinful nature with its passions and desires. Since we live by the Spirit, let us keep in step with the Spirit.

What two things was the apostle Paul setting in opposition here?

How would you define the "sinful nature"?

Below is a chart summarizing the acts of the sinful nature and the fruit of the Spirit, as Paul described them:

Acts of the Sinful Nature	**Fruit of the Spirit**
_____ Sexual immorality	_____ Love
_____ Impurity	_____ Joy
_____ Debauchery	_____ Peace
_____ Idolatry	_____ Patience
_____ Witchcraft	_____ Kindness
_____ Hatred	_____ Goodness
_____ Discord	_____ Faithfulness
_____ Jealousy	_____ Gentleness
_____ Fits of rage	_____ Self-control
_____ Selfish ambition	
_____ Dissensions	
_____ Orgies	

Which acts of the sinful nature can come into play when one is carrying out a dialogue that is *not* Christlike? Put an "x" by each one.

Which fruits of the Spirit do you think are most important when dialoguing with someone who believes differently? Put a check mark by each one.

How does one "crucify" the sinful nature? Write your answer inside the cross.

How does one "keep in step" with the Spirit? Write your answer inside the footprint.

A Wisdom from Beyond Ourselves

Paul's fellow apostle James shared Paul's penchant for emphasizing how Christians have to choose between God's way and the world's way. James did this in terms of "wisdom," and his words should make us think about the kind of wisdom we rely upon when dialoguing with others.

James 3:13-18:

> Who is wise and understanding among you? Let him show it by his good life, by deeds done in the humility that comes from wisdom. But if you harbor bitter envy and selfish ambition in your hearts, do not boast about it or deny the truth. Such "wisdom" does not come down from heaven but is earthly, unspiritual, of the devil. For where you have envy and selfish ambition, there you find disorder and every evil practice.
>
> But the wisdom that comes from heaven is first of all pure; then peace-loving, considerate, submissive, full of mercy and good fruit, impartial and sincere. Peacemakers who sow in peace raise a harvest of righteousness.

What clues do you see that some of James' readers may have been proud of their supposed wisdom?

According to James, what are some kinds of behavior that result from following earthly "wisdom"?

What are some kinds of behavior that result from following heavenly wisdom?

Below is a chart outlining the qualities of earthly "wisdom" and heavenly wisdom:

Earthly "Wisdom"	Heavenly Wisdom
_____ Unspiritual	_____ Humble
_____ Devilish	_____ Pure
_____ Bitterly envious	_____ Peace-loving
_____ Selfishly ambitious	_____ Considerate
_____ Disorderly	_____ Submissive
_____ Evil	_____ Merciful
	_____ Fruitful
	_____ Impartial
	_____ Sincere

Put an "x" beside each of the qualities of earthly "wisdom" that can impact our dialogues.

Place a check mark beside each of the qualities of heavenly wisdom that you think are most important in a dialogue.

What similarities do you see between this passage from the book of James and the earlier passage from the book of Galatians?

What differences do you see?

▶ MEDITATION VERSE

[Jesus said,] "If you love me, you will obey what I command. . . . My command is this: Love each other as I have loved you."

—JOHN 14:15; 15:12

PERSONAL APPLICATION

THE CHOICE BEFORE US

If we were to make a catalog of worldly tactics for dialogue, it might include the following: Make the other person look bad, and yourself look good, even if it means stretching the truth. Try to drive wedges between people. Ignore what's positive in your opponent's motives or opinions. Forget that he is a real human being with an ego that needs to be protected. Engage in ridicule and caricature. Power up on your opponent to try to intimidate her. Rub salt in wounds. Alternate between cold logic and colder innuendo, depending on which seems more effective at the moment. Get personal.

And remember, that's a *partial* listing.

Few of us are so cruel as to do all of those things. But have you not found that it is easy to do some of them in the heat of an argument, even when you never intended to? Let us never forget there lies a choice before us: our way (influenced by messages from the world) or God's way. We have to immerse ourselves in God's truth so that obeying it becomes second nature.

NOTES, QUOTES, & ANECDOTES

The Leading

Some years ago I had lunch at a restaurant with a man who was not a believer. His friends had told me that he was the toughest, hardest-hitting, most autocratic, hardheaded, hardhearted man they had ever met. (With a recommendation like that, I didn't bother to check with his enemies.) Twenty minutes into the meal, I could affirm everything they had said.

We were talking about everything but important things when I felt a leading. The Holy Spirit seemed to whisper to me, "Present the simple truth of Jesus dying for sinners as clearly as you possibly can right now."

I didn't want to do that. I thought I knew for certain what his response would be. But the leading was certainly biblical. It fit my gifts, at least under other circumstances, and it was not in any way self-serving! I had a choice: would I trust God, or would I disobey this leading which clearly seemed to be from Him?

I obeyed. Abruptly changing the subject, I asked, "Would you like to know how Jesus Christ takes sinners to heaven?"

"Pardon me?" said the man.

"Point of information," I said. "Would you like to know how Jesus Christ forgives sinners and takes them to heaven?"

"I guess so," he reluctantly agreed.

So, over dessert, I explained the plan of salvation as plainly and as briefly as I knew how. He asked a few questions. We finished lunch, and I went back to work feeling slightly embarrassed.

Two or three days later I almost fell off my chair when the man called me. He said, "Do you know what I did after our lunch together? I went into my bedroom, got on my knees, and said, 'I'm a sinner in need of a Savior.'"

—BILL HYBELS

IN YOUR CASE

Think about a dialogue you have been engaged in. What aspects of how you have been conducting that dialogue might be worldly?

What qualities of godliness are lacking in your dialogue? (If needed, go back and review the fruit of the Spirit and qualities of heavenly wisdom.)

What are some specific ways you can begin substituting godly attributes for worldly qualities?

How can you tell the difference between doing something out of obedience to God and doing something for your own personal gain?

What might get in the way of your being obedient to God's truth?

What can help to keep you on the path of obedience?

FAITH OVER FEAR

Abandoning what we're used to and trusting that God's way is best can be scary. Yet it can also lead to undreamt-of accomplishments for God's glory.

How do you feel about relying on God instead of yourself when you are engaged in a difficult conversation with another?

In what ways has God proven Himself faithful to you in the past when you've taken a "leap of faith" and trusted Him?

What encourages you now to make the choice to go it God's way in dialogue?

One thing you may find helpful is to remember this: it is *your job* to remain the sort of person who is obedient to the law of love in the midst of conflict; it is *God's job* to work in the heart of the other person for change. Stick to your job. Be who you should be and don't presume to think you can make the other person who he or she should be.

Just be faithful. That's enough.

GROUP ACTIVITY (OPTIONAL)

If you are doing this study with others, get together in a small group and each tell about a dialogue in which you are currently involved. Get input from the others on what "God's way" might be in this dialogue. Try to speak wisdom into each other's situation.

Be encouraging and supportive. Follow up later, if you can.

MY COMMITMENT:

BIG IDEA REVIEW

Having a dialogue that builds bridges means making a choice to do it God's way instead of one's own.

BRIDGE TO GOD

I confess, O Lord, that my thoughts are often tainted with sinfulness from within me and from without. Purify my thoughts, I pray, so that I only want to bear the fruit of the Spirit and live by Your heavenly wisdom. Help me focus on who I should be. Help me remain ever faithful to You out of gratitude for all You've done for me and out of awe for who You are. In Christ's name, amen.

COMING UP

The following study is crucial. It takes an in-depth look at the quality that we have said is most basic to building bridges: love. Don't skip this one!

COMPELLING LOVE

BIG IDEA: It pleases God when our underlying motive in difficult relationships is love.

BIBLE BASIS: 1 Corinthians 13

In 2 Corinthians, Paul wrote, "Christ's love compels us" (5:14). He was talking about the compulsion he felt to carry out his ministry of reconciling sinners to God. But in a broader sense, it is Christ's love that compels His followers to do anything that is of kingdom value, including engaging in a healthy way with others who take a different view. Because Christ has shown us love, we can—indeed, we must—show love to people who disagree with us.

But that brings us to a question: What is love? What does love look like in real life where things can get really messy really fast? The answer appears in another letter written to the Corinthians. There Paul displayed the many facets of *agape* (uh-GAW-pay), that special kind of self-sacrificing love.

Among other things, Paul said, "If I speak in the tongues of men and of angels, but have not love, I am only a resounding gong or a clanging cymbal" (1 Corinthians 13:1). When we dialogue, will we add useless noise to the already deafening clamor of debate, or will we choose love over manipulation and relationship over winning?

Study five helps us think about how to apply attributes of love from 1 Corinthians 13 to the business of building bridges. As we do so, perhaps our love will be "compelling" in another sense — drawing others to us and to Jesus Christ. But even if not, we can know we have been faithful to the God who *is* love (see 1 John 4:16).

BIBLE STUDY

THE MANY FACETS OF CHRISTIAN LOVE

If in the past you have enjoyed the "love chapter" mostly for its beauty, I urge you now to subject it to greater analytic scrutiny, especially as it sheds light on Christlike dialogue.

THE ESSENTIAL ELEMENT

It seems that the early Christian believers living in the Greek city of Corinth were a bit too enamored with the more spectacular spiritual gifts, such as speaking in tongues. Paul took time out from addressing that issue (chapters 12 and 14 of 1 Corinthians) to praise in wonderful poetic fashion the more fundamental heart condition of love (chapter 13). He began by underscoring the uselessness of spiritual gifts and actions without love.

1 Corinthians 13:1-3:

> If I speak in the tongues of men and of angels, but have not love, I am only a resounding gong or a clanging cymbal. If I have the gift of prophecy and can fathom all mysteries and all knowledge, and if I have a faith that can move mountains, but have not love, I am nothing. If I give all I possess to the poor and surrender my body to the flames, but have not love, I gain nothing.

What spiritual gifts and actions did Paul mention as being useless without love?

If Paul were to have added the sentence "If I argue for the truth with impeccable logic and precise clarity, but have not love, I achieve nothing," would that statement have been true? Why or why not?

What do you think makes love the indispensable quality for Christians?

CATALOG OF LOVE'S QUALITIES

Paul moved on to present in rapid-fire fashion many of the characteristics of *agape* love. Each of the key words and phrases is a compact bundle that we can profitably "unpack" to help us in our goal of dialoguing as Christ would.

1 Corinthians 13:4-7:

> Love is patient, love is kind. It does not envy, it does not boast, it is not proud. It is not rude, it is not self-seeking, it is not easily angered, it keeps no record of wrongs. Love does not delight in evil but rejoices with the truth. It always protects, always trusts, always hopes, always perseveres.

Pick one or more of the characteristics of love and describe how someone showed love to you in a way that exemplified those characteristics. (For example, maybe your parents bore with you through a rebellious period in your youth, exemplifying patience.)

In what ways has Christ exemplified some of these qualities of love toward us? (Hint: check out Romans 15:7; Ephesians 5:1-2; Colossians 3:13; Titus 3:3-5; 1 Peter 2:18-19,21-24; 4:1-2; and 1 John 3:16.)

THE PERSISTENCE OF LOVE

Paul concluded his "love chapter" with some words about the enduring nature of love. Love is eternal and love is supreme.

1 Corinthians 13:8-13:

> Love never fails. But where there are prophecies, they will cease; where there are tongues, they will be stilled; where there is knowledge, it will pass away. For we know in part and we prophesy in part, but when perfection comes, the imperfect disappears. When I was a child, I talked like a child, I thought like a child, I reasoned like a child. When I became a man, I put childish ways

---

behind me. Now we see but a poor reflection as in a mirror; then we shall see face to face. Now I know in part; then I shall know fully, even as I am fully known.

And now these three remain: faith, hope and love. But the greatest of these is love.

What echoes do you find here of the first three verses in the chapter?

Why are prophecies, tongues, and knowledge of only temporary usefulness?

What was Paul talking about when he referred to growing up?

What was he talking about when he referred to gaining true sight and full knowledge?

What do you think makes love "the greatest"?

The interruption of the subject of love into the discussion of spiritual gifts should be like the interruption of love into our discussion of dialogue. Love is the basis of what we're discussing. Without love, our dialogue is useless—or worse.

▶◀ NOTES, QUOTES, & ANECDOTES

The Quality and Degree of My Love

John wrote that "God is love" in order to make an ethical point, "Since God so loved us, we also ought to love one another" (I Jn. 4:11). Could an observer learn from the quality and degree of love that I show to others—my wife? my husband? my family? my neighbors? people at church? people at work?—anything at all about the greatness of God's love to me?

—J. I. PACKER

▶◀ NOTES, QUOTES, & ANECDOTES

The Making of a "Love-ist"

Revenge for Israeli bombings and exploitation motivates many terrorist acts. As a Palestinian who lost his home and his father to Israel in 1948, I can understand this passion for revenge because I once burned with it too. I wanted to get a gun and explosives and cross the Jordan into Israel and kill every Jew in sight. Thank God, terrorist weapons were not as easily available then as today. I might have eventually obtained a weapon and set off on a mission of death and destruction, but Christ the Messiah "intercepted" me instead. Only when I surrendered to the King of Kings and the Prince of Peace did the hatred for Jews begin to drain from my heart. Thanks to God's grace, I reached the point in November 1973 where I was able to say on a television and radio interview in Israel, "I love you because of Jesus." Jesus of Nazareth solved my hate problem. He kept me from becoming a terrorist.

—ANIS A. SHORROSH

▶ **MEDITATION VERSE**

Christ's love compels us, because we are convinced that one died for all, and therefore all died. And he died for all, that those who live should no longer live for themselves but for him who died for them and was raised again.

—2 CORINTHIANS 5:14-15

PERSONAL APPLICATION

LOVE IN ACTION

Love is sometimes something you feel. It is always something you do.

It's great when you feel love toward your partner in a dialogue, and that kind of felt love is something that you can, to an extent, cultivate within yourself. But regardless of your emotions, you can always treat the other in a way that is consistent with love.

This sort of love is an act of the will. It is a quality of behavior that Paul defined for us in 1 Corinthians 13 and that Christ lived out for us from the manger to the cross. It is not about demanding rights for oneself but about freely giving to the other. It is something we must strive for as we develop a relationship with someone who disagrees with us.

LOVE EXPRESSIONS

Following are two versions of a chart listing each of the characteristics of love identified in 1 Corinthians 13:4-7.

In the right-hand column of the first chart, fill in ways that Christ has expressed the attributes to you. (If you can't think of an example for all the attributes, that's okay.)

Love . . .	How has Christ expressed these attributes toward you?
Is patient	
Is kind	
Does not envy	
Does not boast	
Is not proud	
Is not rude	
Is not self-seeking	
Is not easily angered	
Keeps no record of wrongs	
Does not delight in evil	
Rejoices with truth	
Protects	
Trusts	
Hopes	
Perseveres	

In the second chart, fill in ways that you can express the attributes of love toward someone with an opposing view. Try to keep an actual individual in mind, and be as specific
as you can.

Love . . .	How can you express these attributes toward someone with an opposing view?
Is patient	
Is kind	
Does not envy	
Does not boast	
Is not proud	
Is not rude	
Is not self-seeking	
Is not easily angered	
Keeps no record of wrongs	
Does not delight in evil	
Rejoices with truth	
Protects	
Trusts	
Hopes	
Perseveres	

GROUP ACTIVITY (OPTIONAL)

LOVE CHECK

Which of the following statements do you think is more often true? Check one.

_____ Feeling loving toward someone results in acting lovingly toward that person.

_____ Acting lovingly toward another results in feeling the emotion of love.

Think back to a recent dialogue with someone who disagreed with you. Where was the needle on your love gauge pointing at that time? To "maximum love"? To "three-quarters loving"? To "half loving"? To "one-quarter loving"? Or to "no love"? Draw a needle pointing to the appropriate position.

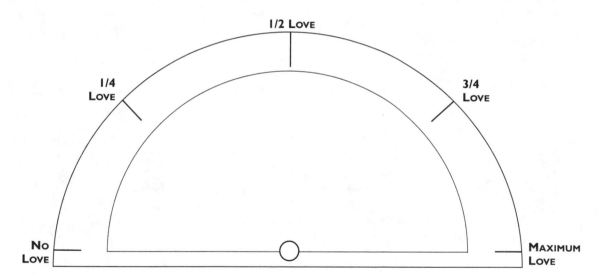

For you, what are the biggest obstacles to having Christlike love for the person you are in dialogue with?

Write as many tips as you can think of for showing love in a dialogue situation. Preferable are tips you have learned through personal experience. Find one other person in the group and trade tips. If you wish, ask for an explanation of them or for the stories behind the tips.

My Commitment:

Big Idea Review

It pleases God when our underlying motive in difficult relationships is love.

Bridge to God

Lord, I know that You are called by the name of Love. May I be known as Christ's disciple because I am known for love. Specifically, when I'm speaking with others, may I so shape my expressions that each word that exits from my mouth reflects love for the other. In Christ's name, amen.

Coming Up

Love for others is possible only as we remember we are sinners who have been forgiven. Building Bridges study six provides a valuable reminder of that truth.

FORGIVEN AND FORGIVING

BIG IDEA: When engaging in a dialogue with someone we consider to be at fault, we must remember that we ourselves are forgiven sinners.

BIBLE BASIS: Matthew 18:23-34; 2 Peter 1:5-9

If you ever encounter a Christian who is acting arrogantly and self-righteously toward an unbeliever with whom he is dialoguing, you can be certain that the Christian has forgotten a simple fact: He is a forgiven sinner himself. On the other hand, when a believer remembers that she has been cleansed from sin, she is free to extend mercy and grace to others, even those who have different views. Now, which Christian would you rather know? Which would you rather be?

Remembering we are forgiven frees us up to love people the way Christ would love them. We would all do well to remember the old adage, "There, but for the grace of God, go I."

With its immeasurably high view of God's holiness and its serious take on human sin, the Bible addresses our present "big idea" at numerous points. We'll look at just two New Testament passages: a parable of Jesus and a portion of Peter's second letter. They'll help us evaluate how we are doing at forgiving others because we ourselves have been forgiven.

BIBLE STUDY

FORGIVENESS RECALLED

The Lord Jesus put an emphasis on forgiving others as no one ever had before. For example, the one line of His model prayer that He felt it necessary to expand upon was the line "Forgive us our debts, as we also have forgiven our debtors" (Matthew 6:12; see verses 14-15). We see this important concept in the two Bible passages that follow.

AN UNMERCIFUL SERVANT

One day during the earthly ministry of Jesus, the disciple Peter wanted to know how many times he was required to forgive someone who sinned against him. Jesus responded with a story that presents forgiveness as a commodity believers are expected to pass along.

Matthew 18:23-34:

> "The kingdom of heaven is like a king who wanted to settle accounts with his servants. As he began the settlement, a man who owed him ten thousand talents was brought to him. Since he was not able to pay, the master ordered that he and his wife and his children and all that he had be sold to repay the debt.
>
> The servant fell on his knees before him. 'Be patient with me,' he begged, 'and I will pay back everything.' The servant's master took pity on him, canceled the debt and let him go.
>
> But when that servant went out, he found one of his fellow servants who owed him a hundred denarii. He grabbed him and began to choke him. 'Pay back what you owe me!' he demanded.
>
> His fellow servant fell to his knees and begged him, 'Be patient with me, and I will pay you back.'

But he refused. Instead, he went off and had the man thrown into prison until he could pay the debt. When the other servants saw what had happened, they were greatly distressed and went and told their master everything that had happened.

Then the master called the servant in. 'You wicked servant,' he said, 'I canceled all that debt of yours because you begged me to. Shouldn't you have had mercy on your fellow servant just as I had on you?' In anger his master turned him over to the jailers to be tortured, until he should pay back all he owed."

In a parable, the key details generally each correspond to some other reality. In this parable, who does the king represent?

Who is represented by the servant whom the king forgave?

Who is represented by the fellow servant?

What do the ten thousand talents (a very large sum) represent?

What do the hundred denarii (a much smaller sum) represent?

If you were to summarize this parable as a one-sentence principle, what would it be?

Grace-Healed Eyes

A prostitute, a wealthy exploiter, a demon-possessed woman, a Roman soldier, a Samaritan with running sores, and another Samaritan with serial husbands—I marvel that Jesus gained the reputation as being a "friend of sinners" like these. As Helmut Thielicke wrote:

> Jesus gained the power to love harlots, bullies, and ruffians. . . . He was able to do this only because he saw through the filth and crust of degeneration, because his eye caught the divine original which is hidden in every way—in *every* man! . . . First and foremost he gives us new eyes. . . .
>
> When Jesus loved a guilt-laden person and helped him, he saw in him an erring child of God. He saw in him a human being whom his Father loved and grieved over because he was going wrong. He saw him as God originally designed and meant him to be, and therefore he saw through the surface layer of grime and dirt to the real man underneath. Jesus did not *identify* the person with his sin, but rather saw in this sin something alien, something that really did not belong to him, something that merely chained and mastered him and from which he would free him and bring him back to his real self. Jesus was able to love men because he loved them right through the layer of mud.

We may be abominations, but we are still God's pride and joy. All of us in the church need "grace-healed eyes" to see the potential in others for the same grace that God has so lavishly bestowed on us.

—PHILIP YANCEY

EFFECTIVE AND PRODUCTIVE

Peter apparently learned the lesson embodied in the parable of the unmerciful servant, for in a letter he wrote many years later, he conveyed a similar sentiment. There is a direct correlation, he indicated, between remembering one's own forgiveness and possessing the Christian graces.

2 Peter 1:5-9:

> Make every effort to add to your faith goodness; and to goodness, knowledge; and to knowledge, self-control; and to self-control, perseverance; and to perseverance, godliness; and to godliness, brotherly kindness; and to brotherly kindness, love. For if you possess these qualities in increasing measure, they will keep you from being ineffective and unproductive in your knowledge of our Lord Jesus Christ. But if anyone does not have them, he is nearsighted and blind, and has forgotten that he has been cleansed from his past sins.

Do you see a progression in the graces Peter mentioned, or do you think it is a random listing?

Which of these graces are most important in a dialogue? Why?

How does one "possess these qualities in increasing measure"?

Why is vision impairment (nearsightedness and blindness) an apt comparison for one who lacks the qualities Peter mentioned?

Why might a person forget the cleansing of his or her sins?

Peter was no longer counting the times he forgave others. Instead, he had shifted his focus to his own sins that had been forgiven. We should do the same.

▶ MEDITATION VERSE

Be kind and compassionate to one another, forgiving each other, just as in Christ God forgave you.

—EPHESIANS 4:32

PERSONAL APPLICATION

THE COMMON GROUND OF SINNERS

In our immaturity, we sometimes make the mistake of forgetting we are forgiven and so come across as self-righteous, having only head knowledge of the truth (information) but failing to have broken and humble hearts (transformation). As we remember the grace and forgiveness God has shown us, the love of Christ should compel us to extend grace, mercy, and forgiveness toward others.

TWO KINDS OF MESSAGES

Take a look at the visual on the following page, showing pregnant women entering an abortion clinic via a gauntlet of pro-life protesters. The volatile issue of abortion will serve us as a sort of case study for different approaches to dialogue.

What do the words on the posters to the left communicate?

What do the words on the posters to the right communicate?

Assuming that all the protesters are Christians, which ones do you think are more likely to have a lively understanding of their own forgiveness before God? Why?

ABORTION CLINIC
REJECTION
ACCEPTANCE
MURDERER
ABORTION KILLS!
BABY KILLER
WE LOVE YOU, WOULD YOU LIKE TO TALK???
I HAD AN ABORTION I UNDERSTAND
I KNOW YOU ARE SCARED
WOMEN CONTEMPLATING ABORTION

Imagine that you are a sixteen-year-old girl who, since becoming pregnant, has been rejected by her boyfriend, criticized by her parents, and left feeling scared and alone. Who would you be more likely to go to: the protesters on the left or those on the right? Or would you ignore both and head on into the abortion clinic? Why?

To Give Forgiveness

Abortion may or may not be an issue over which you are in dialogue. But whatever the issue is, the same principle of dialoguing in the spirit of loving mercy applies.

Do you have an ideological opponent whose faults are very apparent to you? Why do you think that is?

What are some of the sins for which you have been forgiven? (Don't write down the worst ones, if you are afraid someone else will see them, but don't neglect to recall them either.)

If you were to keep in mind the way God has forgiven you, what kinds of specific changes might that mean for your attitude and behavior while dialoguing with others?

GROUP ACTIVITY (OPTIONAL)

If you are in a group studying *Building Bridges,* perform a couple of role-plays with one other person.

In the first role-play, one of you should pretend to be a pregnant young woman who doesn't want to have a child but is hesitant about getting an abortion. The other person should play one of the protesters from the left side of the previous picture. This person is self-righteous, never thinking of himself or herself as a forgiven sinner. The dialogue begins with the pregnant young woman saying to the pro-life protester, "Excuse me, but why does your poster say that?" Take it from there.

In the second role-play, switch roles. This time, the pro-life protester is from the right side of the picture—someone who considers himself or herself a fellow sinner with others. Start the role-play the same way. Where will this one go?

MY COMMITMENT:

BIG IDEA REVIEW

When engaging in a dialogue with someone we consider to be at fault, we must remember that we ourselves are forgiven sinners.

BRIDGE TO GOD

Heavenly Father, give me a clearer sense of the sins by which I have offended Your holiness—not so that I can grovel in what is over and done with but so that I can properly appreciate the grace You have given me. Help me to sense the spiritual need in all whom I meet, however much they may hide it under a hard shell. At the same time, help me to extend mercy to others as You have extended it to me. In Christ's name, amen.

COMING UP

If we are properly humble as people who know we needed—and still need—forgiveness ourselves, we'll be in a position to accept the point of Building Bridges *study seven. That point is that the relationship in a dialogue is more important than the issue under discussion.*

THE MASK OF DECEPTION

BIG IDEA: Contrary to the deception we let ourselves believe, relationships are more important than issues.

BIBLE BASIS: Romans 12:1-2; James 1:19-27

Show me a Christian who is building walls, not bridges, and I will show you a Christian who thinks he's got it all figured out but is actually profoundly deceived.

It's ironic, isn't it? People who are fighting for a particular truth can be overlooking a far more fundamental truth. They are striving to defeat the opposition, but they are failing to obey God in His command to love others. Even if they win their contest, they will most likely be pushing people further away from God. They are deceived in what really matters.

Deception is a mask. It makes a situation look like something it is not. At a costume party, masks can be fun. But in real life, particularly when people are butting heads over a topic they are passionate about, masks can be trouble indeed.

Learning to dialogue with others in the Spirit of Christ means removing any mask of deception. That's what we learn to do in this *Building Bridges* study, examining a couple of key Bible passages and then turning the spotlight on ourselves.

What mask might you be wearing?

BIBLE STUDY

DECEIT TIMES TWO

Deception comes in two varieties: the kind we use to deceive ourselves and the kind others use to deceive us. We deceive ourselves when we ignore what God has taught us in His Word about the primacy of loving others. The world deceives us when it teaches us that prevailing over our opponents, not preserving their worth, is what matters most.

It might seem that we are guilty only in the first case—when we deceive ourselves. But the reality is, we are guilty with both kinds of deception. We always *let* ourselves be deceived. Scripture makes us face up to this distressing truth.

FACE IN A MIRROR

The apostle James wrote a series of practical instructions to Jewish Christians scattered around the Mediterranean world in his day. One perennial issue he addressed was the problem of deceiving oneself by failing to obey what one knows of biblical truth. He could have been talking to us.

James 1:19-27:

> My dear brothers, take note of this: Everyone should be quick to listen, slow to speak and slow to become angry, for man's anger does not bring about the righteous life that God desires. Therefore, get rid of all moral filth and the evil that is so prevalent and humbly accept the word planted in you, which can save you.
>
> Do not merely listen to the word, and so deceive yourselves. Do what it says. Anyone who listens to the word but does not do what it says is like a man who looks at his face in a mirror and, after looking at himself, goes away

and immediately forgets what he looks like. But the man who looks intently into the perfect law that gives freedom, and continues to do this, not forgetting what he has heard, but doing it—he will be blessed in what he does.

If anyone considers himself religious and yet does not keep a tight rein on his tongue, he deceives himself and his religion is worthless. Religion that God our Father accepts as pure and faultless is this: to look after orphans and widows in their distress and to keep oneself from being polluted by the world.

Circle words and phrases in the previous Bible passage that pertain to deceiving oneself.

Underline words and phrases that pertain to *not* deceiving oneself.

In your own words, what is the point of the story about a man who looks in a mirror?

What qualities of speech should people have if they are not deceiving themselves?

What effect does self-deceit have on one's relationship with God?

SQUEEZED INTO A MOLD

James said that deceit is connected with being "polluted by the world." His fellow apostle, Paul, echoed these sentiments when he talked about being conformed to the world's pattern. The Phillips version of the New Testament famously paraphrases the key verse as

"Don't let the world squeeze you into its mold." While we can deceive ourselves by ignoring biblical truth, we can also let ourselves be deceived by others if we allow ourselves to be conformed to society's norms.

Romans 12:1-2:

> I urge you, brothers, in view of God's mercy, to offer your bodies as living sacrifices, holy and pleasing to God—this is your spiritual act of worship. Do not conform any longer to the pattern of this world, but be transformed by the renewing of your mind. Then you will be able to test and approve what God's will is—his good, pleasing and perfect will.

What might conformity to the world look like in a situation where a person is in opposition with someone else? (Hint: check out James 4:1-2.)

What would nonconformity look like in such a situation? (Hint: check out Luke 6:27-36.)

How do you think the renewing of one's mind comes about?

Deceit is always a problem we face. And one of the easiest deceptions is the idea that the people we disagree with don't matter. They matter very much—so much, in fact, that when we are in dialogue with them, preserving their worth should be a higher priority for us than bringing them over to our point of view.

► MEDITATION VERSE

Do not deceive yourselves. If any one of you thinks he is wise by the standards of this age, he should become a "fool" so that he may become wise. For the wisdom of this world is foolishness in God's sight.

—1 CORINTHIANS 3:18-19

PERSONAL APPLICATION

UNDECEIVING ONESELF

The problems of deception that are pointed out in Scripture persist today. Check each box below where you think the person or persons involved are probably suffering from deception.

- ☐ A husband and wife who have withdrawn their love from each other and are considering divorce
- ☐ Church members who are gossiping about another member who is having trouble with her teenage daughter
- ☐ People who have prejudices against members of different races
- ☐ A religious, but self-righteous, political activist who comes across as judgmental of people who hold opposing views
- ☐ A Christian who begins to hate another Christian and takes that person to court
- ☐ People who fight and kill each other over disagreements about religion
- ☐ You in your conflict with another

I hope you checked the first six boxes. I suspect you checked the seventh as well.

What it comes down to right now is *you*. If you are involved in some kind of interpersonal conflict, are you thinking that being "right" is more important than God's command to love one's neighbor as oneself?

DECEPTION COMES HOME

Think about a situation in which you are currently involved in some kind of interpersonal conflict, small or large. (If you can't think of a present example, recall one from the past.) Then answer the following questions.

→ ←
NOTES, QUOTES, & ANECDOTES

The Cold Within

Six humans trapped by happenstance
In black and bitter cold,
Each one possessed a stick of wood,
Or so the story's told.
Their dying fire in need of logs,
The first woman held hers back,
For on the faces around the fire
She noticed one was black.
The next man looking cross the way
Saw one not of his church
And couldn't bring himself to give
The fire his stick of birch.
The third one sat in tattered clothes;
He gave his coat a hitch.
Why should his log be put to use
To warm the idle rich?
The rich man just sat back and thought
Of the wealth he had in store
And how to keep what he had earned
From the lazy, shiftless poor.
The black man's face bespoke revenge
As the fire passed from his sight,
For all he saw in his stick of wood
Was a chance to spite the white.
And the last man of this forlorn group
Did naught except for gain.
Giving only to those who gave
Was how he played the game.
The logs held tight in death's still hands
Was proof of human sin.
They didn't die from the cold without;
They died from the cold within.

—AUTHOR UNKNOWN

What biblical injunctions bearing on your situation make you uncomfortable or do you try to forget?

Why do you think that is?

What messages (spoken or implied) from others have you heard that tell you to win at all costs?

For you, what would it mean to cease being conformed to the world and start being transformed into the likeness of Christ?

How can dialoguing in the Spirit of Christ help you overcome deception in your life?

THE PERSON IS SUPREME

Knowing others personally helps us remember their worth. So think about a person with whom you are in dialogue—what do you know about this person's personal life?

What kind of family life and friendships does he or she have?

What are the needs your dialogue partner is trying to protect by disagreeing with you?

How can you learn more about this person and form a better personal relationship, even a friendship, with him or her?

How can you prioritize the relationship you have with this person?

GROUP ACTIVITY (OPTIONAL)

If you are studying *Building Bridges* as part of a group, get together with two or three others and practice finding out about each other's personal interests. In a casual and non-threatening manner, inquire about each other's families, hobbies, jobs, and other interests. Express your genuine interest in, and appreciation for, what you learn.

All this can be valuable practice for establishing a better relationship with dialogue partners. Critique each other's performance and encourage one another.

MY COMMITMENT:

BIG IDEA REVIEW

Contrary to the deception we let ourselves believe, relationships are more important than issues.

BRIDGE TO GOD

Dear Father, just as Adam and Eve let themselves be deceived in the garden, so I have let myself be deceived over and over again. Forgive me. And more than that, help me to cling to Your Word, which tells me that You love those who love their enemies. Help me to shut my ears to the world's insistence that people are there for me to manipulate. Help me to live in the light of truth and draw others to that truth—and to You. In Christ's name, amen.

COMING UP

Study eight builds on study seven; it teaches us that we are to make meeting others' needs a higher priority than changing their minds. Learn to love your dialogue partner. Be a need meeter.

GRACE BEFORE TRUTH

BIG IDEA: If we want to respond as Christ would with people whose views differ from ours, we must make meeting their needs a higher priority than changing their minds.

BIBLE BASIS: John 3:1-15; 4:7-26; 21:15-19

Have you ever had someone start attacking your viewpoint without first getting to know who you are, what you're dealing with, or how you arrived at your position? How did it feel? We all know it hurts when others treat us as nothing but a potential convert to their way of thinking. We're not just representatives of our viewpoint; we're human beings with needs and concerns all our own.

As followers of the one who gave us the Golden Rule, we should treat our philosophical opponents as we would want to be treated ourselves. We should see them as real human beings who have feelings that can be hurt and who exist in a real-life context out of which they are speaking. If we get to know them on a basic human level, and meet some of their needs as we are able, we may be able to share biblical truth with them in a credible and understandable way.

In *Building Bridges* study eight, we look at ways Christ modeled the principle "grace before truth" and then move on to consider specifically how we can meet the needs of others.

BIBLE STUDY

JESUS: FOUNT OF GRACE AND MERCY

As we examine the following biblical accounts, let us keep in mind that every time we dialogue with someone, we have the same kinds of opportunities Jesus had to extend the grace and mercy that come to us from our heavenly Father.

BY A WELL

In Jesus' day, Jews didn't talk to Samaritans, men didn't talk to women in public, and religious people didn't talk to persons of loose morals. Yet see what ensued when Jesus encountered a promiscuous female Samaritan by a well one noonday.

John 4:7-26:

> When a Samaritan woman came to draw water, Jesus said to her, "Will you give me a drink?" . . .
>
> The Samaritan woman said to him, "You are a Jew and I am a Samaritan woman. How can you ask me for a drink?" (For Jews do not associate with Samaritans.)
>
> Jesus answered her, "If you knew the gift of God and who it is that asks you for a drink, you would have asked him and he would have given you living water."
>
> "Sir," the woman said, "you have nothing to draw with and the well is deep. Where can you get this living water?" . . .
>
> Jesus answered, "Everyone who drinks this water will be thirsty again, but whoever drinks the water I give him will never thirst. Indeed, the water I give

him will become in him a spring of water welling up to eternal life."

The woman said to him, "Sir, give me this water so that I won't get thirsty and have to keep coming here to draw water."

He told her, "Go, call your husband and come back."

"I have no husband," she replied.

Jesus said to her, "You are right when you say you have no husband. The fact is, you have had five husbands, and the man you now have is not your husband. What you have just said is quite true."

"Sir," the woman said, "I can see that you are a prophet. Our fathers worshiped on this mountain, but you Jews claim that the place where we must worship is in Jerusalem."

Jesus declared, "Believe me, woman, a time is coming when you will worship the Father neither on this mountain nor in Jerusalem. You Samaritans worship what you do not know; we worship what we do know, for salvation is from the Jews. Yet a time is coming and has now come when the true worshipers will worship the Father in spirit and truth, for they are the kind of worshipers the Father seeks. God is spirit, and his worshipers must worship in spirit and in truth."

The woman said, "I know that Messiah" (called Christ) "is coming. When he comes, he will explain everything to us."

Then Jesus declared, "I who speak to you am he."

Bible commentators point out that women normally drew water in the evening and used it as an occasion for chatting with one another. The fact that this woman was drawing her water at midday, when only a foreign traveler was present, suggests she was ostracized in her town because of her morals. What, then, do you think it would have meant to her for Jesus to show interest in her and engage her in dialogue?

What common ground did Jesus immediately establish between the two of them?

Identify the ways that the Samaritan woman sought to change the subject. Identify the ways Jesus brought the conversation back on track each time.

What was the woman's need, and how did Jesus meet it?

The Samaritan woman was profoundly changed by her encounter with Jesus. She instantly became an evangelist whose witness led to the conversion of many in her village to faith in Jesus, the Living Water (see John 4:27-42).

A LATE-NIGHT INTRUSION

Jesus' enemies included the Pharisees, those religious experts who thought they were God's favorites because they obeyed the laws scrupulously. Still, at least one Pharisee—a man named Nicodemus—took Jesus seriously as a teacher. Yet probably so that his colleagues would not hear of his interest, he approached the Lord under the cover of darkness.

John 3:1-15:

> Now there was a man of the Pharisees named Nicodemus, a member of the Jewish ruling council. He came to Jesus at night and said, "Rabbi, we know you are a teacher who has come from God. For no one could perform the miraculous signs you are doing if God were not with him."
>
> In reply Jesus declared, "I tell you the truth, no one can see the kingdom of God unless he is born again."
>
> "How can a man be born when he is old?" Nicodemus asked. "Surely he

cannot enter a second time into his mother's womb to be born!"

Jesus answered, "I tell you the truth, no one can enter the kingdom of God unless he is born of water and the Spirit. Flesh gives birth to flesh, but the Spirit gives birth to spirit. You should not be surprised at my saying, 'You must be born again.' The wind blows wherever it pleases. You hear its sound, but you cannot tell where it comes from or where it is going. So it is with everyone born of the Spirit."

"How can this be?" Nicodemus asked.

"You are Israel's teacher," said Jesus, "and do you not understand these things? I tell you the truth, we speak of what we know, and we testify to what we have seen, but still you people do not accept our testimony. I have spoken to you of earthly things and you do not believe; how then will you believe if I speak of heavenly things? No one has ever gone into heaven except the one who came from heaven—the Son of Man. Just as Moses lifted up the snake in the desert, so the Son of Man must be lifted up, that everyone who believes in him may have eternal life."

Jesus' quiet evening, at the end of a long day of ministry, was interrupted by the knock of a man who wanted to talk to Him. In what sense was Jesus' response to the intrusion an extension of grace?

Circle each instance where the word *teacher* or *rabbi* (which means "teacher") appears. Underline the instances where Jesus says, "I tell you the truth." In what sense was truth the common ground between the Pharisee and the Galilean rabbi?

What do you think was Nicodemus's attitude toward Jesus, and what was he seeking?

How would you describe Jesus' attitude toward Nicodemus?

What was Nicodemus's need, and how did Jesus meet it?

Given that Nicodemus helped to bury Jesus after the Son of Man had been "lifted up" (see John 19:39-40), we can be hopeful that this Pharisee received Jesus as his Savior.

AN AFTER-BREAKFAST CONVERSATION

On that terrible night when Jesus was arrested and tried, Simon Peter denied being Jesus' disciple. But later, one morning after the Resurrection, Jesus restored the wayward disciple by giving him a chance to affirm his love for Christ three times—the same number of times he had denied Him.

John 21:15-19:

> Jesus said to Simon Peter, "Simon son of John, do you truly love me more than these?"
> "Yes, Lord," he said, "you know that I love you."
> Jesus said, "Feed my lambs."
> Again Jesus said, "Simon son of John, do you truly love me?"
> He answered, "Yes, Lord, you know that I love you."
> Jesus said, "Take care of my sheep."
> The third time he said to him, "Simon son of John, do you love me?"
> Peter was hurt because Jesus asked him the third time, "Do you love me?"

He said, "Lord, you know all things; you know that I love you."

Jesus said, "Feed my sheep. I tell you the truth, when you were younger you dressed yourself and went where you wanted; but when you are old you will stretch out your hands, and someone else will dress you and lead you where you do not want to go." Jesus said this to indicate the kind of death by which Peter would glorify God. Then he said to him, "Follow me!"

How do you think Peter felt in the presence of Jesus after his triple denial?

In what sense was Jesus' repeated questioning of Peter an act of grace?

Why do you think Jesus responded to Peter's professed love for Him by commanding the disciple to "feed" (serve) Jesus' "lambs" (followers)?

What truth did Jesus convey to Peter?

What new light did Jesus' prediction of Peter's martyrdom throw on Peter's commitment to Jesus?

What do you think his triple affirmation of love for Jesus would mean to Peter in the days to come?

What was Peter's need, and how did Jesus meet it?

Nicodemus, the Samaritan woman, and Peter all had different needs (at least on the surface). But Jesus engaged each in an appropriate conversation and found ways to meet their needs. He used dialogue and common ground to help people realize their true need was for Jesus Himself. He began with grace, and that opened the door for truth.

▶ MEDITATION VERSE

Mercy triumphs over judgment!

—JAMES 2:13

PERSONAL APPLICATION

STARTING ANEW WITH GRACE

Relationships are crucial. It's not fair to dump our version of reality on other people and just write them off if they don't agree. We should get to know them *as persons* and seek to meet their spiritual and other needs as we are able.

Maybe you have failed to put grace before truth when dealing with people in the past. If so, there is forgiveness available to you—and perhaps also the possibility of repairing the damage you have done. Certainly in your current relationships you can start now to love people into the truth as Jesus did.

TRUTH BEFORE GRACE IN THE PAST

Have you ever put truth before grace in dealing with someone who took a position opposite to yours? If so, describe the situation and the results of your actions.

If you have put truth before grace, have you ever asked forgiveness (from God and from the person you hurt)? When and how?

Is it yet possible to make amends to the other person? If so, how?

We can and should regret our past mistakes, but we can also learn from them. Do your best to learn from any mistakes you have made in the past by trying to push your ideas on someone without having

A Love as Never Before

I had been a counselor for thirty-four years when I attended a seminar put on by Accountability Ministries. I had long been convinced that the truth could set my clients free, in accordance with John 8:36. But then, at the seminar I attended, what struck home to me most was the principle of grace before truth. Two days after the seminar, I would get a chance to put that principle into practice.

I had been counseling with a married couple whose relationship had suffered for years as a result of their deep resentment and distrust of one another. The husband's self-righteous condemnation of his wife triggered in her an intense rage that was tearing apart the family, which included two children. During that particular session following the seminar, as I listened to the couple complain about one another yet again, I remembered the principle of grace before truth. With great tenderness and mercy, I began to help the husband see his self-righteousness and the effects of belittling his wife.

Suddenly, realization of the truth hit him deep in his heart. Shedding tears of repentance, he apologized to his wife and asked the heavenly Father for forgiveness.

His wife tearfully forgave him and repented of her rage. She explained to her husband, "For years I have felt that you didn't like me, that there has been something wrong with me, and that caused me to feel deeply hurt. Then I reacted in rage toward you. But now I sense that you accept me for who I am."

The Lord healed this couple's hurt, mistrust, and anger toward one another so completely that they have a new and loving relationship such as they have never experienced before. They now extend toward one another the same grace God has extended to them.

—JEAN ORR

any genuine concern for him or her. If you realize you need to ask forgiveness or take other actions, I encourage you to do so as soon as possible.

GRACE BEFORE TRUTH IN THE PRESENT

Currently, who is one person you would consider your opponent? Write his or her name below:

_____

What do you know about who this person really is? Especially, what needs or problems does he or she have?

How can you form a closer personal relationship with this person? (Think about common ground you share.)

What needs of this other person are you willing to try to meet, if he or she gives you permission? (Consider ways of putting the Golden Rule into practice according to Matthew 7:12.)

What kinds of benefits do you think you might get for yourself by being in a better relationship with this person?

How might you present the truth differently to this person after forming a real relationship with him or her?

Realistically, we don't have time to form a relationship with everyone we may deal with on an issue. But we can't afford not to form relationships with the key people. Before God, commit to putting grace before truth with the people He puts on your heart.

GROUP ACTIVITY (OPTIONAL)

If you are going through *Building Bridges* as part of a group, identify a need you can meet for someone with whom you are in dialogue. For example, you may be in dialogue with a fellow church member who is upset by the changes you have been making in the adult education class you lead. In part, this church member is upset because she has been pushed out of church leadership positions and is feeling unwanted and unappreciated. You could meet her need for feeling valued by asking her help in some area.

Write down a step-by-step process for how you could meet this need in a gracious way. You may want to write down actual words you could use to bring up the subject with your dialogue partner. (This is important, since it is possible to make things worse by seeming to want to put yourself in a one-up position by fixing things for your dialogue partner.)

Trade papers with another member of your study group and read what you see. Then give each other the benefit of your appraisal.

MY COMMITMENT:

BIG IDEA REVIEW

If we want to respond as Christ would with people whose views differ from ours, we must make meeting their needs a higher priority than changing their minds.

BRIDGE TO GOD

Lord, I love Your truth and I want others to love it too! But help me never to be so eager to share the truth that I run right over someone Your Son died for. Open my eyes to others' true situations. Soften my heart to their needs. Help me to show them love and compassion, just as You have shown me. In Christ's name, amen.

COMING UP

In Building Bridges *study nine, we will look at the importance of the listening component of a dialogue.*

QUICK TO LISTEN, SLOW TO SPEAK

BIG IDEA: Those who want to build bridges, and not just win arguments, will listen at least as much as they speak.

BIBLE BASIS: Job 2:11-13; 4:1-2; 32:6,10-12,18-20

A part of being a Christian is being other-minded. And a part of being other-minded, as it relates to our dialogues, is taking the time to listen to what others are saying. And I mean really listening. Not just biding time until an opening to respond presents itself. Not taking the occasion to formulate one's own reply in the most devastating form possible. But actually seeking to understand what the other person is saying and in the process showing respect to him or her.

Knowing how to listen is a skill we will learn in the next *Building Bridges* study. This study, instead, underscores the importance of listening. That might seem simple — why not state it and move on? But how many times have others failed to listen to you? Wasn't it frustrating? We need to learn to listen.

Our helper in this endeavor is the book of Job. Bible students often focus on only the dramatic opening and closing chapters of this book, but here we will be looking at some turning points in the middle section—that lengthy formal dialogue among Job and some of his friends. Let's *listen* to what they have to say to us.

BIBLE STUDY

ON THE ASH HEAP

If you wish to get out your Bible and skim through chapters 1–4 and 32–42 of Job, that may give you a greater comprehension of the study. But the passages quoted below get at the heart of the issue.

THE SILENCE IS BROKEN

In antiquity, a righteous man named Job was struck with a series of unimaginable personal and professional tragedies. With all his family gone (except his wife), Job's only comforters were three friends who showed up at the ash heap where he was sitting, mourning for his losses.

Job 2:11-13; 4:1-2:

> When Job's three friends, Eliphaz the Temanite, Bildad the Shuhite and
> Zophar the Naamathite, heard about all the troubles that had come upon him,
> they set out from their homes and met together by agreement to go and sym-
> pathize with him and comfort him. When they saw him from a distance, they
> could hardly recognize him; they began to weep aloud, and they tore their
> robes and sprinkled dust on their heads. Then they sat on the ground with
> him for seven days and seven nights. No one said a word to him, because they
> saw how great his suffering was. . . .
>
> Then Eliphaz the Temanite replied:
> "If someone ventures a word with you, will you be impatient?
> But who can keep from speaking?"

What was the motive of the three men in coming to visit Job?

What were some things the visitors did right?

After the week of silence, Job spoke first. In essence, he said he wished he had never been born (chapter 3). That's the speech to which Eliphaz replied by launching into his own first speech.

What do you think was Eliphaz's attitude upon starting to speak?

Twenty-eight more chapters pass as we listen to Job and the three friends go around and around. One gets the odd feeling, when reading the speeches, that the men were talking past each other. No one budged. No one changed another's opinion. Essentially, the three friends all said: "Job, your sin caused these sufferings to come upon you; admit it." And in effect, Job replied: "I didn't do anything wrong; I don't know why this happened to me!"

ENTER ELIHU

Throughout the long interchange that went on among Job and the three men, there apparently was another individual sitting by as silent auditor. This younger man, Elihu, spoke up when the other three friends gave up trying to convince Job of his guilt before God. He began by stating why he hadn't spoken before and why he was ready to talk now.

Job 32:6,10-12,18-20:

> I am young in years,
>
> and you are old;
>
> that is why I was fearful,
>
> not daring to tell you what I know. . . .
>
> I say: Listen to me;
>
> I too will tell you what I know.
>
> I waited while you spoke,
>
> I listened to your reasoning;
>
> while you were searching for words,
>
> I gave you my full attention.
>
> But not one of you has proved Job wrong;
>
> none of you has answered his arguments. . . .
>
> I am full of words,
>
> and the spirit within me compels me;
>
> inside I am like bottled-up wine,
>
> like new wineskins ready to burst.
>
> I must speak and find relief;
>
> I must open my lips and reply.

What was Elihu's motive for waiting so long to speak?

What was his motive for starting to speak now?

What attitude do you pick up from Elihu—was he humble or proud? Upon what clues do you base your opinion?

What was Elihu feeling while waiting to speak? What does this say about him?

Have you ever been in a position where you felt like you had words bottled up inside of you and you just had to speak your mind? Describe one such situation.

In what ways is Elihu a positive example for us? In what ways is he a negative example?

Unfortunately, Elihu's speech (chapters 32–37) would prove essentially no different from the others and consequently no more effective than theirs were. It would take the entrance of yet another conversation partner—this one from beyond the clouds—to silence Job and inspire in him a true submission to God (38:1–42:6).

▶ MEDITATION VERSE

Everyone should be quick to listen, slow to speak and slow to become angry, for man's anger does not bring about the righteous life that God desires.

—JAMES 1:19-20

PERSONAL APPLICATION

THE ART OF LISTENING

The three friends, Eliphaz, Bildad, and Zophar, sat in silence for a week, showing sympathy for Job's loss. Elihu waited to speak until his elders had finished their turns. In both cases, these men may have held their tongues only because they were observing a custom in their culture (and in the case of Elihu, we know he could hardly wait to spill his ideas). Nevertheless, they serve as a reminder to us that we have to listen as well as speak.

In terms of its linguistic roots, the word *dialogue* means "two words." There are *two* speakers and *two* listeners in every dialogue—or at least there should be. A good dialogue is one in which each participant gets to say what he wants and is heard out by the other. It's the art of verbal give-and-take.

When the subject of a dialogue is one that people are passionate about, it's easy for them to close their ears and open their mouths. That's when the words tumble on top of each other, the volume rises, and real communication slips out the door. And that's why we have to drill a single thought into our minds: *we have to listen!*

WHY LISTEN?

Have you ever known someone who was a bad listener? If so, how did talking with that person make you feel?

How does talking with a good listener make you feel?

What benefits do you see in listening?
In the ear illustration, list as many as occur to you.

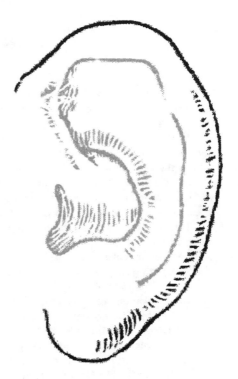

HOW TO BEGIN TO LISTEN

How hard is it for you to keep quiet and stay
focused on what the other person is saying when
you are in dialogue?

What makes listening hard for you?

Who is the best listener you know? What can you learn from that person?

In what other ways might listening be a learnable skill?

What might help you remember to listen when you are engaged in a dialogue?

NOTES, QUOTES, & ANECDOTES

A Little Listening

A pastor was aware of a New Age bookstore in his community that had a coffee shop inside. He saw it as a great opportunity to get acquainted with people who had not received Jesus Christ and to work on preparing his sermon.

One day, as he was about to leave the bookstore, he approached the checkout counter and asked the clerk, "What is your opinion of Christians?"

As the clerk observed the religious titles of the books the pastor was purchasing, his response to the question was "Oh, they're okay; they're fine."

Convinced he hadn't heard the truth, the pastor pushed the books aside, looked the clerk in the eyes, and asked, "Now, what do you *really* think of Christians?"

This time the clerk gave his honest answer: "I think they are rude, arrogant, obnoxious, and inconsiderate. And they treat me like I'm a bad person."

The pastor replied, "Jesus isn't like that." He then began to share with the clerk how Jesus treated the Samaritan woman at the well, the woman caught in adultery, and the sinful woman who anointed Jesus' feet. The pastor explained that Jesus didn't turn them away because they were sinners. Instead, He loved and accepted them by speaking the truth in love, while never condoning their sin.

Excited by this new revelation, the clerk told the pastor that the owner of the bookstore (who was also a city councilman) needed to hear this message. The next morning, the pastor listened attentively while the owner shared his negative views of Christians. When the man finished talking, the pastor began to share Jesus' love and acceptance of the sinful woman who wiped his feet with her tears in front of Simon the Pharisee, as told in Luke 7:36-50.

After their dialogue, the pastor invited the man to a Sunday service at his church and asked if he would share with the entire congregation his thoughts on how people claiming to be Christians are perceived by people who are not Christians. The man accepted the invitation, and the pastor let him speak on Sunday to the entire congregation. When he finished sharing, the pastor prayed for the man. With tears in his eyes, the councilman looked out at the congregation and said, "If all of you would treat people in this city the way your pastor has treated me, you could turn this city around."

A little listening can go a long way.

—JEFF ROSENAU

GROUP ACTIVITY (OPTIONAL)

If you are studying *Building Bridges* in a group, get together with another group member. Take turns telling each other a story that lasts between three and four minutes (time it with a watch). It can be a story you make up or a real-life story. Either way, it should be full of a lot of specific details.

When you're finished telling your story, quiz your listener about details of the story. For example, if you're telling a story about your dog, ask your listener about the breed of your dog (which you mentioned once). This will serve as a check on your partner's listening comprehension.

Switch places, and you listen as the other tells a story for three to four minutes. How good will your comprehension be?

This is a lighthearted reminder that listening is important and can be hard work.

MY COMMITMENT:

BIG IDEA REVIEW

Those who want to build bridges, and not just win arguments, will listen at least as much as they speak.

BRIDGE TO GOD

I know that You have endowed each person with dignity, Lord, creating us in Your image. Help me to remember that dignity when I am talking with someone whose views I disapprove of. Remind me to show that person respect by taking the time to understand what he or she is saying and to respond only when it is appropriate. In Christ's name, amen.

COMING UP

The following Building Bridges *study builds on this one. It tells us how to listen, namely, listening to really understand and not so as to judge the other.*

LISTENING WITH LOVE

BIG IDEA: If we are motivated by love, we will really listen to others and will not judge or condemn them.

BIBLE BASIS: Matthew 7:1-5; Romans 2:1-4

We all listen. Few of us listen well.

If we plan on dialoguing with people who have views in opposition to our own, we must develop the heart and skills of a good listener. These attitudes and abilities do not come naturally. But they are invaluable. When we are listening well, we have little time to label and judge.

Stereotyping, judging, and criticizing people whom we perceive as different from ourselves, instead of taking the time to build a relationship with them through dialogue, creates barriers to effective evangelism and to unity among God's people. Maybe that's why the Bible writers spent so much of their time on the evil (not to mention hypocrisy) of condemning others.

In this *Building Bridges* study, we look at two powerful passages about judging others, one from the Gospels and one from the Letters. We also get practical about effective listening and speaking.

BIBLE STUDY

THE WEAPON THAT CUTS THE WIELDER

What kind of witness do Christians have as the world takes note of how many of our marriages end in divorce? What kind of appeal do our churches have to spiritual seekers if we are always arguing over local church practices or denominational differences? How will others be drawn to Christ if they observe Christians responding in a self-righteous manner over issues such as abortion, sexual immorality, and even prayer?

One problem is that we're not listening to others. We're talking. And when we're talking, we're all too often using words designed to cut others down. We let others know just what we think of them. In the process, we fail to love our neighbors as ourselves.

You'd think we'd know better. After all, the Scriptures make it plain that judgmentalism is a sword that turns upon the one who wields it. Jesus taught us that; so did Paul. In fact, they speak as if with one voice.

OF SPECKS AND PLANKS

The Sermon on the Mount may well be the most familiar—and least heeded—sermon in history. That's because it is so challenging to our sinful human tendencies. One key topic in the sermon is that of judging others, as the Pharisees judged less religiously observant people in their day.

Matthew 7:1-5:

> "Do not judge, or you too will be judged. For in the same way you judge others, you will be judged, and with the measure you use, it will be measured to you.
>
> Why do you look at the speck of sawdust in your brother's eye and pay no attention to the plank in your own eye? How can you say to your brother,

'Let me take the speck out of your eye,' when all the time there is a plank in your own eye? You hypocrite, first take the plank out of your own eye, and then you will see clearly to remove the speck from your brother's eye."

What can the one who judges expect to happen to him or her?

What does the speck/plank analogy tell us about the relative significance of the sin in the lives of the two "brothers"?

Why do you think people tend to notice others' minor sins while ignoring their own major ones?

Practically speaking, what does "taking the plank out of one's own eye" mean?

NOTES, QUOTES, & ANECDOTES

Love and Unlove

"God is love," that is, love for others, and the moment we fail in love towards another, we put ourselves out of fellowship with God—for God loves him, even if we don't. . . .

Now we all know what Jesus meant by the speck in the other person's eye. It is some fault which we fancy we can discern in him; it may be an act he has done against us, or some attitude he adopts towards us. But what did the Lord Jesus mean by the plank in our eye? I suggest that the plank in our eye is simply our unloving reaction to the other man's speck. Without doubt there is a wrong in the other person. But our reaction to that wrong is wrong too! The speck in him has provoked in us resentment, or coldness, or criticism, or bitterness, or evil speaking, or ill will—all of them variants of the basic ill, unlove.

—ROY HESSION

How does removing one's own "plank" qualify one to help another deal with his or her "speck"?

The Rebound Effect

The apostle Paul made it clear that one thing all people—Jews and Gentiles—share is our guilt before God. We are all sinners. That's why he said we should leave judgment to God.

Romans 2:1-4:

> You . . . have no excuse, you who pass judgment on someone else, for at whatever point you judge the other, you are condemning yourself, because you who pass judgment do the same things. Now we know that God's judgment against those who do such things is based on truth. So when you, a mere man, pass judgment on them and yet do the same things, do you think you will escape God's judgment? Or do you show contempt for the riches of his kindness, tolerance and patience, not realizing that God's kindness leads you toward repentance?

What points of similarity do you see between this passage and the previous one (Matthew 7:1-5)?

What reason(s) did Paul give for not judging others?

Would you say that people tend to underestimate the wickedness of being judgmental? If so, why is that?

What does one sinner's being judgmental of another say to God, in effect?

The opposite of speaking with the intent to judge is listening with a motivation of love. Before we move to judge, we must first withdraw our love—and withdrawing love is always wrong.

► **MEDITATION VERSE**

The entire law is summed up in a single command: "Love your neighbor as yourself." If you keep on biting and devouring each other, watch out or you will be destroyed by each other.

—GALATIANS 5:14-15

PERSONAL APPLICATION

EFFECTIVE LISTENING AND SPEAKING

Listening with love is not easy. Thankfully, though, it is something we can learn how to do.

LISTENING GUIDELINES

When in the role of listener in a conversation, try to learn why the other person believes the way he or she does so that you can understand and prayerfully consider that point of view. As you do so, keep in mind these guidelines:

1. Maintain eye contact. Focus all your attention on the one talking.
2. Use body language that communicates you are paying attention, such as leaning toward the other person at times. Smile and nod when appropriate.
3. At the same time, be relaxed, indicating you are comfortable with the other person.
4. As needed, ask questions to clarify what the other is saying or to get more details. These should be open-ended questions, using the words *who, what, when, where, why,* and *how,* rather than yes-no questions. Ask these questions one at a time. Never use them in an attempt to manipulate the other, but only out of an honest desire to understand better.

5. Try to pick up on underlying feelings, messages, and needs. Probe gently, if necessary.
   - "It seems you might be feeling . . . "
   - "Is what you're really saying . . . "
   - "I get the sense . . . "

6. From time to time, rephrase what the other has just said to you for clarification.
   - "Let me see if I understand . . . "
   - "Do I hear you saying . . . "
   - "Would it be correct to say your point is . . . "

7. React to what the other is saying; don't just sit there. Reacting positively could be as simple as nodding or saying *"Mm-hmm."* Or it could be more involved, such as giving praise and encouragement when warranted.

Think back to the most recent time when you were discussing a potentially touchy issue with someone who held a view different from your own. In light of the listening guidelines, what would you say you did well in the conversation?

What areas of weakness can you work on to prepare for the next time?

SPEAKING GUIDELINES

When it is your turn to speak, try to help meet the needs of the person you are talking to without compromising your obedience to God. These guidelines will assist you:

1. Maintain eye contact. Focus all your attention on the one with whom you are talking.
2. Be relaxed, indicating you are comfortable with the other person.
3. Keep the volume of your voice down; never raise your voice in anger.

4. Make your points clearly and succinctly, offering sound reasons for your beliefs and avoiding sidetracks.

5. Maintain a reasonable tone, indicating that you are discussing the matter, not quarreling.

6. Graciously allow the other person to interrupt with a question for clarification.

7. Show respect to the other person, choosing your words carefully. Never ridicule the other or condemn that person for his beliefs or behaviors.

Again think back to the most recent time when you were discussing a potentially touchy issue. In light of the speaking guidelines, what would you say you did well in the conversation?

What areas of weakness can you work on to prepare for the next time?

GROUP ACTIVITY (OPTIONAL)

If you are studying *Building Bridges* in a group, get together with two other people to practice your listening and speaking skills. Here's how to do it: For the purposes of this exercise, choose a subject you are knowledgeable about but not passionately interested in. (An example might be whether Christians should go to R-rated movies.) Take one

---

NOTES, QUOTES, & ANECDOTES

The Liberty of Christ

A spiritually minded person will never come to you with the demand—"Believe this and that"; a spiritually minded person will demand that you align your life with the standards of Jesus. We are called to present liberty for the conscience of others, not to bring them liberty for their thoughts and opinions. And if we ourselves are free with the liberty of Christ, others will be brought into that same liberty—the liberty that comes from realizing the absolute control and authority of Jesus Christ.

Always measure your life solely by the standards of Jesus. Submit yourself to His yoke, and His alone; and always be careful never to place a yoke on others that is not of Jesus Christ. It takes God a long time to get us to stop thinking that unless everyone sees things exactly as we do, they must be wrong. That is never God's view. There is only one true liberty—the liberty of Jesus at work in our conscience enabling us to do what is right.

Don't get impatient with others. Remember how God dealt with you—with patience and with gentleness. But never water down the truth of God. Let it have its way and never apologize for it. Jesus said, "Go . . . and make disciples . . ." (Matt. 28:19), not, "Make converts to your own thoughts and opinions."

—OSWALD CHAMBERS

side of the issue and have a second person take the other side. The third person should evaluate you, using the rating sheets that follow. The rating scale is from 0 to 10 (0 meaning "failed entirely to do this" and 10 meaning "exhibited this skill as well as anyone could"). Remember, the purpose of this exercise is not to "win" at the discussion; it is to practice *how* to discuss. If you wish, the three of you can keep trading places so that each one can play the role of listener, speaker, and evaluator at least once.

This is only practice, but it is preparing you for real-life discussions in which the stakes may be very high.

Listening Skills of _____ (name)	Rating (0-10)	Comments
Maintaining eye contact		
Showing attentiveness		
Being relaxed		
Asking open-ended questions		
Probing for underlying feelings, messages, and needs		
Rephrasing what the other said for clarification		
Reacting positively to the speaker		
Listening skills total:		

Speaking Skills of _____ (name)	Rating (0-10)	Comments
Maintaining eye contact		
Being relaxed		
Keeping volume low		
Maintaining a reasonable tone		
Making points clearly and succinctly		
Showing respect for the listener		
Allowing the listener to interrupt for clarification		
Speaking skills total:		

My Commitment:

Big Idea Review

If we are motivated by love, we will really listen to others and will not judge or condemn them.

BRIDGE TO GOD

Dear Lord, I know You are the Judge of all, including this sinner. Forgive me for the times I have ignored my own culpability and focused on the wrongs of others. Help me to replace judging with loving. Make me ever more able to really hear what people are saying and even more committed to sharing truth with them only as I have earned the right to do so. I trust You to guide and bless my attempts. In Christ's name, amen.

COMING UP

In Building Bridges *study eleven we look deeper into one key aspect of Christlike speech. It's what the apostle Paul called "gently instructing" others.*

THE ART OF GENTLE INSTRUCTION

BIG IDEA: We should never quarrel with others but instead gently instruct them when the opportunity arises.

BIBLE BASIS: 2 Timothy 2:14-17,23-26 and other selected New Testament verses

Standing up for the truth does not mean attacking others. A dialogue is not a battle. In any good dialogue a time will come when we will get to present our viewpoint, but then we must do it with the gentleness that comes from never forgetting the priority of the relationship. If we have as our motive the greatest good for the other person, how can we be other than gentle?

There is an art to instructing gently. Jesus knew how to instruct gently, and He did it without compromising truth. (The only people Jesus ever got angry with were the religious leaders of the day, who didn't practice what they preached and weren't really listening to what He said.) We can learn this art of gentle instruction through attention and practice.

But first we must be convicted, deep down in our souls, that we really *must* be gentle. Only as we understand this will we act as we should when finding ourselves in a high-pressure dialogue situation. And Scripture helps us learn that lesson. In this *Building Bridges* study we will look at several key passages and then seek to apply the principle of gentleness to our own situations.

BIBLE STUDY

WORDS SPOKEN SOFTLY
The importance of gentle speech is one of those threads that make up Scripture's beautiful tapestry of godliness. Let us trace out this one bright thread.

THE SERVANT OF THE LORD
The apostle Paul had placed his protégé Timothy in a key position in Ephesus, and in his last letter before execution, the older man wrote to instruct the younger. For one thing, Paul warned Timothy not to let himself get embroiled in the semantic arguments that had become a pastime among some in the Christian community.

2 Timothy 2:14-17,23-26:

> Warn them before God against quarreling about words; it is of no value, and only ruins those who listen. Do your best to present yourself to God as one approved, a workman who does not need to be ashamed and who correctly handles the word of truth. Avoid godless chatter, because those who indulge in it will become more and more ungodly. Their teaching will spread like gangrene. . . .
>
> Don't have anything to do with foolish and stupid arguments, because you know they produce quarrels. And the Lord's servant must not quarrel; instead, he must be kind to everyone, able to teach, not resentful. Those who oppose him he must gently instruct, in the hope that God will grant them repentance leading them to a knowledge of the truth, and that they will come to their senses and escape from the trap of the devil, who has taken them captive to do his will.

What effects of quarreling are detailed here?

How is "correctly handl[ing] the word of truth" different from "quarreling about words"?

How would you define godless chatter and why do those who indulge in it become more and more ungodly?

What qualities is the Lord's servant expected to embody?

What motivation and hope should the Lord's servant have when interacting with an opponent?

NOTES, QUOTES, & ANECDOTES

What Gentleness Means

"Blessed are the gentle, for they shall inherit the earth" (Matt. 5:5).

Immediately, we may get a false impression. We think, "Blessed are the weak for they shall become doormats." In our rough-and-rugged individualism, we think of gentleness as weakness, being soft, and virtually spineless. Not so! The Greek term is extremely colorful, helping us grasp a correct understanding of why the Lord sees the need for servants to be gentle.

It is used several ways in extrabiblical literature:

- A wild stallion that has been tamed, brought under control, is described as being "gentle."
- Carefully chosen words that soothe strong emotions are referred to as "gentle" words.
- Ointment that takes the fever and sting out of a wound is called "gentle."
- In one of Plato's works, a child asks the physician to be tender as he treats him. The child uses this term "gentle."
- Those who are polite, who have tact and are courteous, and who treat others with dignity and respect are called "gentle" people.

So then, gentleness includes such enviable qualities as having strength under control, being calm and peaceful when surrounded by a heated atmosphere, emitting a soothing effect on those who may be angry or otherwise beside themselves, and possessing tact and gracious courtesy that causes others to retain their self-esteem and dignity. Clearly, it includes a Christlikeness, since the same word is used to describe His own makeup: "Come to me, all who are weary and heavy laden, and I will give you rest. Take my yoke upon you and learn from me, for I am gentle and humble in heart, and you shall find rest for your souls" (Matt. 11:28-29).

—CHARLES R. SWINDOLL

A POTPOURRI OF GENTLENESS TEACHINGS

Many passages from the Bible echo Paul's words to Timothy about gentle instruction. Below is a sampling of five such passages from different books of the New Testament.

Ephesians 4:2:

> Be completely humble and gentle; be patient, bearing with one another in love.

Philippians 2:3-4:

> Do nothing out of selfish ambition or vain conceit, but in humility consider others better than yourselves. Each of you should look not only to your own interests, but also to the interests of others.

Colossians 4:6:

> Let your conversation be always full of grace, seasoned with salt, so that you may know how to answer everyone.

2 Timothy 4:2:

> Preach the Word; be prepared in season and out of season; correct, rebuke and encourage—with great patience and careful instruction.

1 Peter 3:15-16:

> But in your hearts set apart Christ as Lord. Always be prepared to give an answer to everyone who asks you to give the reason for the hope that you have. But do this with gentleness and respect, keeping a clear conscience, so that those who speak maliciously against your good behavior in Christ may be ashamed of their slander.

Go back through the five brief passages and underline or highlight the words and phrases that describe the manner with which Christians are to dialogue with others. Which of these strikes you the most, and why?

If you were to think of these passages as painting a composite picture of the Christian in dialogue, what would you say that picture looks like?

Gentleness is a trait that many of us find hard to apply to our speech. Maybe that's why the Scriptures are so insistent on it. The Lord's servant must not quarrel but instead must gently instruct.

▶ MEDITATION VERSE

A gentle answer turns away wrath, but a harsh word stirs up anger.

—PROVERBS 15:1

PERSONAL APPLICATION

CULTIVATION OF GENTLENESS

Many aspects of Christlike dialogue could be used cynically as a tool to manipulate one's dialogue partner. Gentleness is a case in point. One could use a soothing tone and kind words to try to pull others around to one's own way of thinking against their wills. One *could* do that. But that is not what we are talking about.

We're talking about being gentle with others because we respect them and love them and want what's best for them. We want them, as well as ourselves, to accept the truth, because that's best for us, but our gentleness is not a technique in service of a selfish goal of getting compliance. It's gentleness for gentleness's sake. Or rather, gentleness for the Lord's sake.

Gentleness is a quality we can cultivate, if we are willing. As it becomes a habit, we will become known for our gentle spirit. We will be bridge builders.

GUIDELINES FOR GENTLE INSTRUCTION

Gentleness is not a technique; it is a godly attitude and fruit of the Holy Spirit. But I've found that certain guidelines are generally helpful in instructing others gently. Become a friend to someone who has an opposing view by:

1. Accepting that person for who he or she is.
2. Finding common ground.
3. Humbly considering the other person as better than yourself and looking not only to your own interests but also to that person's interests.
4. Giving the other the freedom to speak the truth as he or she sees it.
5. Asking questions to learn what the other person believes rather than assuming you know it.
6. Being open to the possibility of your being the one who (at least in part) is wrong and is in need of repentance. (Be teachable.)
7. Having a sincere desire and hope that the Holy Spirit will lead both of you to a knowledge of the truth and that God will grant repentance to whoever is in need of repenting.

What is your reaction to this list of guidelines? Would you add any guidelines to, or subtract any from, the list?

In what ways might these guidelines help you in your dialogues?

THE GIFT OF GENTLENESS

Think of a recent incident when you were treated harshly by someone who disagreed with you. How did it feel to be on the receiving end of that sort of treatment?

If you were to ask the people who know you best how gentle they consider you to be in general, what do you think they would say?

What images come to your mind when you think of gentleness (a mother with her baby, for example)? Draw simple pictures of the images that occur to you.

What gets in the way of your being more gentle with people who think differently from you?

In what specific ways could you be more gentle in your dialogues?

GROUP ACTIVITY (OPTIONAL)

If you are studying *Building Bridges* in a group, get together with one other person. Take turns performing an instruction exercise.

Choose a message that you want to communicate. For example, the message could be that teens should not disrespect their bodies by getting body piercing (you do not have to pick an issue that you are actually concerned about). Make this point to your partner in two different ways: first, very harshly, then with true gentleness. As a parent to your teenager, start, for example, by yelling, "What's that ring doing in your eyebrow? You look like a hoodlum. Get out of this house!" In the second attempt you will practice gentle instruction.

Switch places with your partner, so that you are on the receiving end of two versions of a message.

You can have fun with this exercise, but it has a serious point. It shows us that there are different ways of saying things. We need to learn how to instruct gently.

MY COMMITMENT:

BIG IDEA REVIEW

We should never quarrel with others but instead gently instruct them when the opportunity arises.

BRIDGE TO GOD

Lord, You have treated me gently, though I have deserved Your wrath. Help me likewise to treat others gently, speaking the truth to them in ways that will not hurt them but will nurture them so that they might draw nearer to You. In Christ's name, amen.

COMING UP

Our course reaches its finale in study twelve with the subject of speaking truth in love. This is what it's all about!

SPEAKING THE TRUTH IN LOVE

BIG IDEA: Building bridges requires us to remain faithful to godly truth while treating our dialogue partners with unfailing love.

BIBLE BASIS: Isaiah 59:1-4; Ephesians 4:11-16

To many people, what this *Building Bridges* study (and indeed the whole *Building Bridges* course) teaches may seem paradoxical. They think that if they are to be loving to others, they have to compromise their beliefs. Or they think that if they are to hold on to truth, they will inevitably alienate their dialogue partners.

What the Bible teaches us to do is to hold on to *both* truth *and* love. It's not easy. But nothing less is required of us if we want to be faithful to scriptural teaching on how we are to treat people who differ from us on issues. (And in my experience, a surprising number of times this approach leads to both a great relationship and success in agreeing on the truth!)

Our scriptural study passages this time show us two things: (1) what can happen if people abandon both truth and love, and (2) what can happen when people hold on to both truth and love. In the personal application section, we get to some practical guidelines for dialogue. Now we are building bridges for real!

BIBLE STUDY

TRUTH AND FALSEHOOD

Following are two contrasting Scripture passages. In the first, look for what *not* to do; in the second, look for the attitude you *should* have in Christlike dialogue.

LYING LIPS

The history of Israel records many sad periods when the people fell away from obedience to God. The prophet Isaiah spoke to his people during one such period, condemning their wrongdoing. What's interesting, for our purposes, is the prominent role that the misuse of speech played in the Israelites' sin.

Isaiah 59:1-4:

> Surely the arm of the LORD is not too short to save,
> nor his ear too dull to hear.
> But your iniquities have separated
> you from your God;
> your sins have hidden his face from you,
> so that he will not hear.
> For your hands are stained with blood,
> your fingers with guilt.
> Your lips have spoken lies,
> and your tongue mutters wicked things.
> No one calls for justice;
> no one pleads his case with integrity.
> They rely on empty arguments and speak lies;
> they conceive trouble and give birth to evil.

According to this passage, what does sin do to one's relationship with God?

What kinds of wrongful speech do you see detailed here? Highlight or underline key words and phrases.

What other kinds of sin seem to be closely allied to improper argument?

GROWING UP INTO CHRIST

In a number of places in his writings, Paul emphasized the importance of unity within the body of Christ. One of those places, Ephesians 4, provides the context for the principle that is fundamental to building bridges rather than walls: speaking the truth in love.

Ephesians 4:11-16:

> [Christ] gave some to be apostles, some to be prophets, some to be evangelists, and some to be pastors and teachers, to prepare God's people for works of service, so that the body of Christ may be built up until we all reach unity in the faith and in the knowledge of the Son of God and become mature, attaining to the whole measure of the fullness of Christ.
>
> Then we will no longer be infants, tossed back and forth by the waves, and blown here and there by every wind of teaching and by the cunning and craftiness of men in their deceitful scheming. Instead, speaking the truth in love, we will in all things grow up into him who is the Head, that is, Christ. From him the whole body, joined and held together by every supporting ligament, grows and builds itself up in love, as each part does its work.

How can the diversity of ministry roles (apostles, prophets, and so on) produce the unity of which Paul was speaking?

What imagery do you see in this passage that expresses spiritual growth and maturity? Underline key words and phrases.

What imagery do you see that expresses unity? Circle key words and phrases.

How did Paul describe the effects of false teaching?

What is the effect of speaking the truth in love?

There are any number of opportunities before us to use our God-given gift of speech in ungodly ways, and we have many different words for them: *lying, slandering, quarreling, gossiping, belittling,* and so on. But the *right* way of speaking is to *tell the truth* and to *tell it in love.*

▶ MEDITATION VERSE

Instead, speaking the truth in love, we will in all things grow up into him who is the Head, that is, Christ.

—EPHESIANS 4:15

PERSONAL APPLICATION

GUIDELINES FOR DIALOGUE

Through many years of learning about dialogue and striving to build bridges, I have developed a set of guidelines that can be helpful in initiating dialogue. Actually, I have developed *two* sets of guidelines (one being a variation of the other), depending on the situation. The first set of guidelines is for two people who desire to mature in Christ. The second set of guidelines is for one person who desires to mature in Christ and one who doesn't share that desire but is willing to peacefully discuss differences.

It is important to keep in mind that people are at different levels of spiritual maturity, so don't have unrealistic expectations of yourself or others. You are not there to convert the other person to your way of thinking. Remain humble and teachable, open to patiently bearing with others in love and allowing the Holy Spirit time to work in people's lives, including yours.

I present these sets of guidelines for your use. But keep in mind that these are *only* guidelines. Don't think you have to follow each step. Try to initiate dialogue in the simplest way possible. For example, with my sons, I simply gave them the freedom to speak the truth in love and confront me any time they thought I was wrong, as long as they did it respectfully (see "Making an Adjustment").

As you read these guidelines, you'll see that they synthesize many of the principles taught in previous *Building Bridges* studies and provide a mechanism for "speaking the truth in love."

GUIDELINES FOR TWO MATURING CHRISTIANS

If the partners in a dialogue are both Christians who wish to honor God and to mature in Christ, they have common ground in regard to their objectives and the authority for their beliefs. Here are some guidelines they can use:

1. If one of the parties is in authority over the other, it is imperative that the person in authority give the one under authority the freedom to speak the truth in love without being criticized or punished for it.

NOTES, QUOTES, & ANECDOTES

Making an Adjustment

My two sons, Rob and Travis, are grown up now, but when they were college students home on summer vacation, one of my greatest joys was working with them in our job of adjusting property claims. We were a team and had different responsibilities.

As we were working one day, I asked them, "What don't you like about me as a dad?" and "How can I be a better dad?"

In their responses they implied that I was a controller and that they were not being given much say as to the roles and responsibilities each of them should have while performing their work. But they made these points in a way that plainly expressed their respect and love for me as their dad.

That night I gave them the responsibility of deciding each person's role for the next day. I said they could choose their own assignments and assume the role they felt most qualified to do and enjoyed the most. I also let them tell me what my assignment would be. The next day was enjoyable for everyone and turned out to be even more efficient than had been our previous arrangement.

Think you can't learn from your kids? You can if they speak the truth in love—and if you listen in love.

The following are some questions I encourage parents to ask of their spouse and children, as Christlike dialogue begins at home.

- In what ways have I been too busy with other priorities? What changes can I make toward building a more meaningful relationship with you?
- In what ways have I been self-centered? What changes can I make toward becoming more other-minded?
- So that I can repent and ask forgiveness, can you think of times I have withdrawn my love when I didn't get my own way?
- What other sins or weaknesses do you see in my life that are keeping me from being a more godly spouse or parent?
- I want to serve and honor you above myself, and consider your interests as important as my own. Will you kindly remind me when I fail to do so?

—JEFF ROSENAU

---

2. They should agree on a common goal, namely, to mature in Christ and build a relationship that glorifies God.

3. They should identify common ground for the dialogue. This does not need to be the issue or concern that they are in disagreement about. It may be anything they have in common that will help them build a relationship prior to discussing their differences.

4. Prior to the discussion, the two should agree to forgive each other if one offends the other in any way as they dialogue. Also, they should agree that when the session is over, they will love and accept each other even if they still disagree.

5. Each person should be open to the possibility of being wrong and deceived in certain ways.

6. Prior to beginning each dialogue, they should agree to pray a prayer along these lines: "Father, whatever is in our lives that You want to take out or change, help us to recognize it and yield to You. Show us the truth. Let us see any deception in our lives that You want us to be free of."

7. They should agree to give one another the freedom to speak the truth in love as each perceives it, without interruption from the other person (except to ask questions for clarification). The underlying motive must be love for God and love for each other and a desire to learn what changes, if any, God wants them to make that will help both of them mature in Christ.

8. They should listen and learn from each other but not attempt to persuade the other person to their point of view or assume the other is wrong just because he or she doesn't agree.

9. It is not important that they agree with each other. What is important is that they agree with God, mature in Christ, and maintain love and respect for each other despite differences.

10. The two should agree to leave the other person's decision, and the consequences of that decision, between the person and God (unless church discipline needs to be properly administered in love under the authority of the church by following the principles in Matthew 18:15-17).

11. They should close by praying and asking God to grant both of them repentance as needed, leading whoever is deceived to a knowledge of the truth for God's glory and their well-being.

If you are in dialogue with another Christian who, like you, is interested in dialoguing God's way, how can these guidelines improve your conversations?

GUIDELINES FOR A MATURING CHRISTIAN AND ONE OTHER

When one partner in a dialogue is not a Christian (or at least is not a Christian who wants to mature in Christ and to please God with the dialogue), a slightly different set of guidelines must apply. But as long as both are willing to discuss the issue peacefully, dialogue can go on. The maturing Christian still has the responsibility of dialoguing in a Christlike manner. You'll notice both similarities and differences between the following set of guidelines and the set of guidelines listed previously.

1. If one of the parties is in authority over the other, it is imperative that the person in authority give the one under authority the freedom to speak the truth in love without being criticized or punished for it.

2. They should agree on a common goal, namely, to discuss differences and come to a knowledge of the truth.

3. They should identify common ground for the dialogue. This does not need to be the issue or concern that they are in disagreement about. It may be anything they have in common that will help them build a relationship prior to discussing their differences.

4. Prior to the discussion, the two should agree to forgive each other if one offends the other in any way as they dialogue. Also, they should agree that when the session is over, they will not be critical or judgmental of each other even if they still disagree.

5. Each person should be open to the possibility of being wrong and deceived in certain ways.

6. If both persons are willing, they should pray before each dialogue, asking God to bring them both to a greater knowledge and understanding of truth.

7. They should agree to give one another the freedom to speak the truth in love, as each perceives it, without interruption from the other person (except to ask questions for clarification). Furthermore, they should be open to replacing their opinion of truth with the real truth if they are wrong.

8. They should listen and learn from each other but not attempt to persuade the other person to their point of view or assume the other is wrong just because he or she doesn't agree.

9. It is not important that they agree with each other.

If you are in dialogue with someone who is not seeking to mature in Christ (maybe a nonChristian or a worldly Christian), how can these guidelines improve your conversations?

Who is God leading you to initiate Christlike dialogue with so that they, like you, can come to know Jesus Christ for who He really is? Begin soon to build bridges. This is how lives are changed, including yours!

GROUP ACTIVITY (OPTIONAL)

If you are studying *Building Bridges* with a group, spend extended time in prayer with your group praying about the specific dialogues that each is involved in. Use this time to labor in prayer on behalf of one another, asking God's help to make the dialogues occasions where the truth is spoken in love.

MY COMMITMENT:

BIG IDEA REVIEW

Building bridges requires us to remain faithful to godly truth while treating our dialogue partners with unfailing love.

BRIDGE TO GOD

Dear Lord, I thank You for the things I have learned about Christlike dialogue in this course. I pray that You will use these insights to help me build bridges and not walls with other people. Help me to speak the truth in love to all I meet. In Christ's name, amen.

GROUP LEADER GUIDELINES

Building Bridges, Not Walls is a flexible Bible study program on dialoguing in the Spirit of Christ. It can be used either individually or in a group. If it's going to be used in a group, anyone with a little gifting in the area of small-group leadership should be able to lead the studies successfully. This appendix is designed to give some basic information to help the group leader.

If you are to be the leader of a group studying Building Bridges, Not Walls, I recommend you look at yourself more as a facilitator than as a teacher. You need to make sure the group gets organized and that it covers the material in an effective fashion. But you don't have to be the "expert."

The studies themselves contain the key Bible passages as well as questions and activities. This appendix contains some general guidelines for leading your group. With God's blessing, that should be all you need!

SCHEDULE

The Building Bridges program includes twelve studies. You should plan to cover them all, but when you cover them is up to you.

You may wish to spread the studies out over a long period of time. For example, if you are the teacher of an adult education class in a church, you could choose to do one study per week for twelve weeks. That should work well for you if your church education program is organized on a quarterly basis.

On the other hand, you may wish to cover the studies as an intensive seminar. One possible scenario in that case is to lead the seminar on a Friday night and Saturday. Here's how you might choose to schedule your seminar time:

SUGGESTED SEMINAR SCHEDULE

Friday night

6:30-6:45—Welcome and introduction
6:45-7:30—Study 1
7:30-7:45—Break
7:45-8:30—Study 2
8:30-9:15—Study 3

Saturday

8:30-8:45—Welcome and announcements
8:45-9:30—Study 4
9:30-10:15—Study 5
10:15-10:30—Break
10:30-11:15—Study 6
11:15-12:00—Study 7
12:00-1:00—Lunch
1:00-1:45—Study 8
1:45-2:30—Study 9
2:30-2:45—Break
2:45-3:30—Study 10
3:30-4:15—Study 11
4:15-4:30—Break
4:30-5:15—Study 12
5:15-5:30—Wrap-up

Either way (led once a week or all at once), *Building Bridges, Not Walls* will serve as an effective curriculum to help your group members learn how to dialogue in the Spirit of Christ. Make your plans, then go for it!

TEACHING TIPS

Basically, leading a *Building Bridges* study is a process of introducing the topic, reading Bible passages, discussing Bible study questions, and then moving on to deal with personal application questions. You can throw in additional elements as they occur to you.

Here are some tips you may want to consider:

Gather your supplies. Make sure that you and each group member has a copy of *Building Bridges, Not Walls* as well as a Bible and a pen or pencil. Additional supplies you may wish to have on hand include a flip chart or whiteboard, markers, and sheets of paper.

Treat the study as a spiritual exercise, not just a learning experience. Pray before the studies. Allow students to bring up prayer requests and to pray for one another.

Keep the session focused. This is a balancing act. Sometimes a discussion going off onto a sidetrack may be God's leading. But for the most part, you'll want to make sure that the study stays close to the Big Idea and keeps moving along so that you cover all the important material by the time you have to quit.

Choose key questions and rework them for your group as necessary. The questions in *Building Bridges, Not Walls* studies are generally aimed at the individual. You may need to restate them to make them appropriate for group discussion. Of course, you can come up with your own questions too.

Follow good discussion practices. To make sure everyone gets the most out of the time, try to draw out the quiet ones and restrain those who are prone to monopolize the conversation. Keep the discussion light and conversational.

Vary the routine. Most of the group time will be spent in a question-and-answer format. But add an activity into the mix from time to time to touch on different learning styles. Each study includes one optional group activity. You may choose to use this activity, if it fits in with your plans. You can also come up with your own activities. For example, you might create role-plays that your group members can use to practice the skills they are learning.

Use small groups skillfully. If your group is over eight persons, break the group down into even smaller groups occasionally when you want participants to be able to discuss a matter at greater length. These smaller groups can also be valuable at prayer time.

Model the principles you are teaching. Your group study is a type of dialogue. Make sure that you put relationships above issues, instruct gently, find common ground, and so on.

Don't push anyone to do anything that's uncomfortable. For example, if a group member has poor reading skills or is very shy, don't ask him or her to read a Scripture passage out loud. If a particular question is highly personal, don't ask anyone to answer it out loud. Use your common sense and sensitivity to make these judgment calls.

Bring in your own experiences. Tell personal stories if they are relevant to what you are teaching, even if those stories don't always reflect well on yourself. The group members will appreciate your transparency.

Other than that, be as creative as you like! If you have a TV and VCR available, you could play a movie clip that illustrates a point. You could bring in a guest speaker who has a fascinating story to tell that is relevant to one study. Or you could create a PowerPoint presentation to display a series of guidelines. The possibilities are limited only by your imagination.

ACCOUNTABILITY GROUPS

The time will come when your group has been through the last *Building Bridges* study. Does growth in Christlike dialogue have to end then? No! Not if you help your group members form accountability groups.

An accountability group is simply a small group in which the members volunteer to keep in touch and encourage one another in their attempts to dialogue as Christ would and build relationships that are honoring to God. Consider inviting your group members to form such groups (six people maximum) at the end of your group study time. Just think of the impact Christ's disciples can have if we truly become known by our love for one another.

The Mutual Accountability Covenant (page 139) describes the responsibilities of accountability group members. Photocopy the covenant and hold a little ceremony in which group members sign the covenant. Conclude with prayer.

MUTUAL ACCOUNTABILITY COVENANT

Out of my desire to mature in Christ, I agree and commit before God to:

1. Give people within my accountability group the freedom to "speak the truth in love" to me. They may discuss any concerns or differences they have with me for the purpose of helping us all grow in unity and in our knowledge of Christ. (John 17:20-21; 1 Corinthians 1:10; Matthew 18:15; Ephesians 4:13-15)

2. Dialogue directly with anyone with whom I experience conflict, rather than gossip about them or quarrel with them. This means I will not share with others that which I should say directly to the person with the opposing view. It also means that when I dialogue with that person, I will, with God's grace, do so in the Spirit of Christ. (Proverbs 26:20-21; 2 Timothy 2:24-26)

3. Practice the biblical principles learned through *Building Bridges* training and follow its guidelines for dialogue as appropriate to the situation.

4. Avoid judging others and being self-righteous. I understand that people are at different levels of spiritual maturity, and I will give others freedom to grow spiritually without withdrawing my love from them during the process. (Matthew 7:1-5; Romans 2:1-4; 14:1,4)

5. Edify others as I dialogue by encouraging, building up, and praying with and for people who disagree with me. (Hebrews 3:13; Ephesians 4:29; James 5:16)

6. Practice forbearance and overlook minor offenses, patiently bearing with others in love. (Ephesians 4:2-3; Colossians 3:13; Romans 12:10; 15:1-2,7)

7. Gently and humbly, yet firmly, hold others in my group accountable if they violate this commitment. (Galatians 6:1)

I agree to practice this covenant in my relationships with the following people:

_____

_____

_____   _____
Signature   Date

SOURCES AND PERMISSIONS

The following are the sources of excerpts used in the "Notes, Quotes, & Anecdotes" features.

"A Window to His Glory" (page 23) is taken from Paul David Tripp, *War of Words: Getting to the Heart of Your Communication Struggles* (Phillipsburg, N.J.: P&R Publishing, 2000), p. 192.

"The Power of Lamblikeness" (page 30) is taken from Roy Hession, *The Calvary Road* (London: Christian Literature Crusade, 1950), pp. 98-101. Used by permission.

"Learning to Love by Learning to Obey" (page 50) is taken from C. S. Lewis, *Mere Christianity* (New York: Macmillan, 1980), p. 83.

"The Leading" (page 54) is taken from Bill Hybels, *Too Busy Not to Pray*, 2d ed. (Downers Grove, Ill.: InterVarsity, 1998), pp. 165-166.

"A Love That Would Not Give Up" (page 60) is taken from Ken Sande, *The Peacemaker: A Biblical Guide to Resolving Personal Conflict* (Grand Rapids, Mich.: Baker, 1997), pp. 202-203.

"The Quality and Degree of My Love" (page 62) is taken from J. I. Packer, *Knowing God* (Downers Grove, Ill.: InterVarsity, 1973), p. 127.

"The Making of a 'Love-ist'"(page 62) is taken from Anis A. Shorrosh, *Islam Revealed: A Christian Arab's View of Islam* (Nashville: Nelson, 1988), pp. 284-285.

"Grace-Healed Eyes" (page 70) is taken from Philip Yancey, *What's So Amazing About Grace?* (Grand Rapids, Mich.: Zondervan, 1997), p. 175.

"What Christians Must Learn" (page 72) is taken from David C. Reardon, *Making Abortion Rare: A Healing Strategy for a Divided Nation* (Springfield, Ill.: Acorn, 1996), p. 6.

"Love and Unlove" (page 109) is taken from Roy Hession, *The Calvary Road* (London: Christian Literature Crusade, 1950), pp. 55, 83-84. Adapted by permission.

"The Liberty of Christ" (page 113) is taken from Oswald Chambers, *My Utmost for His Highest* (Grand Rapids, Mich.: Discovery House, 1992), May 6. Used by permission.

"What Gentleness Means" (page 119) is taken from Charles R. Swindoll, *Improving Your Serve: The Art of Unselfish Living* (Waco, Tex.: Word, 1981), pp. 104-105.

ABOUT THE AUTHOR

JEFF ROSENAU is founder and president of Accountability Ministries, a Colorado-based organization with a national and international reach that teaches biblical principles to prepare God's people to dialogue in the Spirit of Christ. He has presented the material contained in *Building Bridges, Not Walls* to leadership and laity at numerous churches and to leadership at a number of parachurch organizations, including Advocates International, Christian Legal Society, Colorado Christian University, Crisis Pregnancy Centers, International Student Connection, Peacemaker Ministries, The Christian and Missionary Alliance, and The Navigators.

A graduate of Western Michigan University, Jeff resides in Colorado. He has two grown sons, Rob and Travis, a daughter-in-law, Sandi, and a grandson, Brevin.

To learn more about Accountability Ministries, log on to www.accountabilityministries.org. If you'd like to book Jeff Rosenau as teacher of the *Building Bridges, Not Walls* seminar for your church or organization, contact him in one of the following ways.

Write:
    Accountability Ministries
    14046 E. Stanford Circle, I-6
    Aurora, CO 80015

Call:
    (303) 690-9671

E-mail:
    jlr@accountabilityministries.org

LEARN HOW TO RESPOND TO THOSE AROUND YOU.

A Public Faith

This challenging book gives a much-needed call to action without politicizing the church. Charles Drew's balanced approach gives Christians a solid, biblical foundation for making decisions and taking a stand without stepping on toes.

by Charles Drew
1-57683-215-5
5 ¹/₂ x 8 ¹/₂
Paperback

Steering Through Chaos

Ethics matter. This book contrasts over 2500 years of Western thought on vice with Jesus' beatitudes. Based on Trinity Forum's exclusive seminars, this book draws from their successful leadership-building materials.

by Os Guinness
1-57683-158-2
7 ³/₈ x 9 ³/₈
Paperback

Minding Your Emotions

How are you feeling? In this practical guide, the author explains how understanding your feelings can lead to spiritual growth, personal healing, and joyful living. As you progress, learn to help those around you heal as well.

by Steve Shores
1-57683-174-4
5 ¹/₂ x 8 ¹/₂
Paperback

To get your copies, visit your local bookstore, call 1-800-366-7788, or log on to www.navpress.com. Ask for a FREE catalog of NavPress products. Offer #BPA.